Cannabis

Table of Contents

Introduction

The future of the medical world, the future of our own health, lies on our basic right to use anything that grows, anything that the soil provides us with, as a healing agent. Why should cannabis be excluded from this mandate? Why shouldn't we use something that has been used for more than 10,000 years as a natural way to alleviate pain and suffering?

The politics that surround cannabis are incredibly complex but there is one thing that is incredibly simple – the truth. Cannabis has long been known to have healing benefits, as well as providing fuel, food, shelter and clothing when all its byproducts are used.

As I will tell you later on, the human body was actually designed to be receptive to the active compounds, or cannabinoids in cannabis but our medical industry and the governments do not want you to make use of them. Indeed, they will go to the long and expensive lengths of imprisoning anyone found to be using or even in possession of cannabis without a medical card.

The thought that these people want you to believe is that cannabis contains no benefits in terms of healing whatsoever but even they can't argue with thousands of years of history. The real issue comes down to the fact that the FDA must approve anything that can treat, cure, prevent, and even diagnose a disease or medical condition. They are not going to give cannabis FDA approval, only drugs that have more side effects than is safe, side effects that often make you feel far worse than the original condition, drugs that see you given a prescription for yet another drug to cure the side effects.

The pharmaceutical agents who supply these drugs refuse to acknowledge that the body has its own healing abilities, preferring to go with the premise that they can give you a drug for anything – so long as it isn't cannabis.

What I am going to tell you is exactly what cannabis is. I will tell you of the whole list of health benefits that this humble weed possesses, how you can grow your own and what you can do with it.

Please keep in mind that cannabis is an illegal drug unless you carry an official medical marijuana card, in which case, you must ensure that you follow the rules of your specific State carefully.

Chapter 1:
History of Cannabis

C annabis has perhaps one of the longest and most colorful histories ever read about. From prehistoric times, to Viking ships and Ancient China, cannabis has been in use for thousands of years, across the whole globe, for a whole range of different things. Before we look deep into its past, it is important that you lean the difference between the two subspecies of cannabis. The first is the Cannabis sativa plant, better known as marijuana and it is this one that has the psychoactive properties. Cannabis sativa L is better known as hemp and it contains no psychoactive properties. Hemp is actually used in the manufacture of many things that are in use today – rope, clothing, oil and fuel, not to mention a variety of cloths.

Cannabis indica is another variety of the plant that is psychoactive and it was first identified by Jean-Baptiste Lamarck, a French naturalist. A final species, cannabis ruderalis, was named by a Russian botanist called D E Janischevisky in 1924.

It is believed that the cannabis plant first originated in central Asia, growing and evolving on the steppes in what are now known as Southern Siberia and Mongolia. We can trace cannabis back as far as 12,000 year and this puts the plant firmly among the list of the world's oldest cultivated crops. We can even go so far as to say that the crop most likely flourished on the sites of the prehistoric hunters and gatherers, in their nutrient rich dump sites.

The Kurgan burial mounds, located in Siberia, have also turned up a number of burnt cannabis seeds that can be dated back to about 3000 BC. Tombs of high-ranking people in Siberia and in Xinjiang in China, dated back to around 2500 BC were found to have large amounts of mummified marijuana, the psychoactive kind.

The Ancient Chinese were found to have used psychoactive marijuana and hemp and the first medicinal use can be dated back to 4000 BC. It was used during surgery to anesthetize peoples and there are tales that the Chinese Emperor Sheng Nung used it in 2737 BC. Whether the story is true or whether the Emperor was a real person or fictional has been the subject of much debate, especially since the first real Emperor of a unified China came into the world much later than Shen Nung was reportedly alive.

Cannabis moved from China to Korea in around 2000 BC, taken there by coastal farmers and, between 2000 and 1000 BC, cannabis arrived in the South Asian subcontinent. This was at a time when the area was inhabited by an invading army of Aryans, an army that spoke a language described as archaic Indo-European. The drug entered India, widely used and hailed as one of the "five kingdoms of herbs", which are claimed to be able to release a person from feelings of anxiety.

Asia to Europe

Between 2000 and 1400 B, cannabis arrived in the Middle East most likely used by a nomadic Indo-European group known as the Scythians. It is these people who are also likely to have transported the drug to the Ukraine and Southeast Russia, as the Scythians were now to have occupied both for many years. Cannabis made its way to Germany by way of Germanic tribes and from there, during the 5th Century Anglo-Saxon invasions, the drug made its way to the United Kingdom. Seeds have also been uncovered in Viking ship remains that can be dated to the middle of the 9th century.

Through the next few centuries, cannabis spread across the world, through Africa and eventually arriving in South America in the 19th Century. From there, it continued its journey, eventually abetting to North America.

From Europe to USA

After a long journey, the drug finally landed in the United States of America at the start of the 20th Century. It came to the southwest via Mexico when the immigrants flooded out of the country in 1910 to 1911, during the Mexican Revolution.

Much of the early prejudice against the drug came about through racist fears of the people that smoked it. In those days, the Mexicans were blamed for using cannabis, committing crimes against properties, tempting children and carrying out murder sprees. Much of the prejudice likely came from stories printed in the local newspapers.

Laws in America never determined the difference between Cannabis sativa and Cannabis Sativa L, resulting in the actual plant being made illegal in 1915 in Utah. By 1931, another 28 states had followed suit. Harry Aslinger was the very first FBN commissioner (Federal Bureau of Narcotics) in 1930 and he made many efforts to try to make cannabis illegal in every single state. The drug fell foul of the Marijuana Tax Act in 1937, giving the DEA (Drug Enforcement Agency) the power to regulate it. This resulted in it becoming a criminal act to possess a cannabis plant. This regulation covered the entire country.

Today, cannabis is still a Class 1 controlled substance, up there with the likes of heroin, cocaine and LSD. This is an indicator that the drug has a very high potential for misuse and addiction, as well as an indicator that the drug is not safe to use at any level and does not demonstrate any medical benefits.

With the rest of this book, I will show you just how safe cannabis is to use and all the benefits it brings in terms of medical use.

Chapter 2:
What is Cannabis?

Cannabis or marijuana comes from the leaves, seeds, stems and dried flower heads of the hemp plant, Cannabis sativa. This plant has been used for many hundreds of years to make seed oil, fibers, for the seed itself, for medical use and in a recreational sense.

Cannabis sativa contains THC – tetrahydrocannabinol. This psychoactive chemical targets certain receptors in the brain cells. These receptors are called cannabinoids, the receptors I mentioned earlier that are predisposed to accept cannabis. Within seconds of smoking cannabis, the THC is detectable in the blood stream.

There has been a lot of research carried out on THC and it has been irrefutably shown that it has analgesic effects, providing mild to moderate relief from pain. The reason for this is because it changes the release of transmitters in the spinal cord.

THC has also been shown to stimulate the appetite, which is why users often get a case of "the munchies". It brings on a state of relaxation and also affects the senses of sight, smell and hearing. In some people THC cause fatigue and in others, it has to be shown to temper down aggressive behavior. Other studies show that THC also has antiemetic qualities – it reduces feelings of nausea and vomiting.

Medical marijuana is now legal in 23 US States, with more looking likely to follow suit. It is used to treat muscle spasms, chronic pain, sleep disturbance, nausea and anorexia. It does not come under government standardization, which means that its potency and the ingredients in it are not known.

In terms of being a recreational drug, cannabis has a number of slang terms that it is known by, including dope, pot, hash, weed, grass and hashish. It comes in a range of different forms for recreational use, including:

- Resin

- Unprocessed – stems, leaves, flowers, all dried

- Powder

- Oil

Cannabis is a dioecious plant. There are some plants with male reproductive systems and others with female reproductive systems. The female plant would need to be pollinated by the male plant before it can reproduce. The female plant then starts to flower and after pollination, it goes on to produces seeds.

Of course, there are types of Cannabis that do not fall in the criteria mentioned above. For instance, Sinsemilla is one example of a female cannabis plant that can reproduce without the need for marijuana plants with male reproductive systems. They can produce seedless flowers and these flowers are known to be highly potent.

Monoecious Condition (Hermaphrodite)

Depending on the varieties of cannabis that are available, different variations of marijuana may be reproduced. There is a condition wherein both flowers bred by the same plant contain female and male reproductive systems so it can pollinate without the need for another plant.

The flower may also be exposed to wide variety of natural conditions; this can make the flower last longer on the plant than others. This condition is called a hermaphrodite condition. Plants that occur in this way are considered to be Monoecious.

There is also another possible outcome that may occur when male plants produce enough pollen to pollinate the female plants that are nearby. When the female plants become pollinated, they produce seeds. The seeds will eventually mature and will cause the female plant die. There are two things that can happen with the seeds that have come from the cannabis plant:

- Seeds may drop to the ground and will grow into new marijuana plants.

- Seeds can also be gathered and will then be used to harvest other plant products or hemp seed oil.

Feminized Cannabis Seeds

It has already been mentioned earlier that some seeds are produced by plants that have the hermaphrodite condition.

Since this is highly sought after, there are different methods in which this can be achieved:

lowered the IOP (intraocular pressure) when it was smoked. This was shown in people who had normal pressure in their eyes and in those who had glaucoma. The effects produced by cannabis can help to slow the disease down, preventing a sufferer from going blind.

It Can Help to Reverse Carcinogenic Effects from Tobacco

Cannabis can help improving the health of the lungs. A study that was published in 2012 showed that cannabis has no negative effect on lung function and can help to increase capacity. Researchers tested the lung function of more than 5000 young adults, in research carried out over 20 years into heart disease risk factors. While those who smoked tobacco products did lose lung function over the course of time, those who smoked cannabis displayed a marked increase.

It could be that the increase in capacity is down to the user taking deeper breaths to ensure the drug is inhaled fully, rather than being down to any therapeutic chemical that may be present in cannabis. Research is ongoing in this area.

It Can Help with Epilepsy

Cannabis has been shown to help prevent seizures in epilepsy suffers. This came from a study that was published in 2003. Cannabis extract was given to epileptic rats, along with synthetic cannabis and the seizures were banished for around 10 hours. Cannabinoids like THC bind to the brain cells that work to control relaxation and regulate excitability; the epileptic rats were sent into a state of relaxation, stopping the seizures from being able to happen.

It can Help Decrease the Symptoms of Dravet's Syndrome

Dravet's Syndrome is a severe seizure syndrome, a syndrome that a young child called Charlotte Figi suffers from. During research for a documentary on cannabis, the Figi family were interviewed and stated that hey se medical cannabis to treat their daughter. The strain they use is very low in THC and is high in cannabidiol. The syndrome also causes severe delays in development and, according to the documentary, the child's seizures have decreased significantly since using the medical cannabis. At one stage, she was having more than 300 seizures every week; now it's down to one a week. More than 40 children in the same US state are using the same cannabis strain for their seizures and all of them are reporting that their seizures are becoming fewer and farther apart.

The doctors responsible for recommending the medical cannabis say that it is the cannabidiol in the plant that works

– it binds to the brain cells, lessening excessive brain activity, thus cutting the cause of the seizure. However, it must be noted that a hospital in Florida who specializes in Dravet's Syndrome does not endorse the drug for use in treating seizures, and neither to the Drug Enforcement Agency or the American Academy of Pediatrics

It Can Help to Stop the Spread of Cancer

Cannabidiol, or CBD, has been shown to help stop the spread of cancer, according to a report in 2007, issued by the California Pacific Medical Center.

According to the report, CBD actually switches off a gene by the name of Id-1, stopping cancer in its track. Cancer spreads because the cells make significant numbers of the Id-1 gene, more than they do of the non-cancerous cells, thus hastening its journey through the body.

The Center based their study on breast cancer cells that showed high levels of Id-1 and then treated them with the CBD. Following the treatment, the expression of Id-1 had reduced and did not spread as aggressively as before the treatment. Some studies that have been carried out in the US, Israel and Spain also suggest that cannabis compounds can also kill of cancer cells altogether, although research into this is ongoing.

It Can Help to Decrease Anxiety

Users of medical cannabis claim that the drug has helped to suppress feelings of nausea and to relieve pain and these are the two main side effects of chemotherapy. According to a report from the Harvard Medical School in 2010, the drug helps to reduce levels of anxiety, making it a likely reason why the drug works. The user would have an improved mindset and mood and the drug also has sedative properties when taken in low doses. On the other side of the coin, too high a dose can induce high levels of anxiety and paranoia.

It Can Help to Slow Alzheimer's Disease

A study published by the Scripps Research Institute suggests that cannabis can help to slow down progression of the disease. The study was published in 2006, saying that THC, which is the active compound in the drug, slows down the speed at which amyloidal plaque forms and it does this by blocking the enzyme responsible for making the plaque in the brain. The plaque, left to form at normal speed, will kill of the brain cells, this causing Alzheimer's disease.

It Can Help to Ease Pain from Multiple Sclerosis

According to a report in the Canadian Medical Association Journal, cannabis can help to ease the pain caused by multiple sclerosis. 30 patients were studied, each of them suffering from very painful muscle contractions. None of the patients showed any response to other forms of treatment but when given cannabis to smoke for a few days, their pain had significantly lessened.

This is because THC binds to the receptors in muscles and nerves to help control the pain. There are other studies that say THC can help to control the actual spasms and contractions n the muscles.

It can Help with Other Muscle Spasms

Reports also suggest that cannabis can help with other muscle spasms as well. One teenager suffers from diaphragm spasms that have not responded to any treatment, including strong medications but, on using a medical strain of cannabis, his symptoms have lessened quite significantly. The condition he suffers from is called Myoclonus Diaphragmatic Flutter, also called Leeuwenhoek's Disease. The symptoms are a constant spasming of the abdominal muscles, spasms that are painful and cause trouble with speaking and breathing.

The cannabis calms these attacks down almost straightaway because they calm down the muscles in the diaphragm. **It Can Help with Hepatitis C Treatments**

The treatment for a person with Hepatitis C is not very nice and there are many side effects to the treatment – aches in the muscles, depression, and a loss of appetite, nausea and fatigue. These side effects can go on for many months and may people find that, because of them, they are not able to finish their course of treatment.

Once again, cannabis comes to the rescue. According to a study published in 2006, 86% of those who used cannabis actually completed their treatment course and found that they had much lower instances of side effects. This is compared to 29% of those who did not take cannabis completing their course.

As well as reducing the side effects, the cannabis also seems to have improved the effectiveness of the treatment itself. 54% of those who took the cannabis showed that their viral levels lowered and stayed low, compared to only 8% of those who did not take the cannabis.

It can Help with the Treatment of Inflammatory Bowel Disease

Studies have suggested that those with inflammatory bowel diseases like ulcerative colitis and Crohn's Disease could gain enormous benefit from using cannabis. Research carried out in 2010 showed that the chemicals in the cannabis, like the Cannabidiol and THC, interact with the cells that play a vital role in the function of the gut and the immune responses. According to the research, compounds in the body that are similar to THC make the gut more permeable, thus allowing more bacteria to find its way in. The cannabinoids in the actual plant block the cannabinoids in the body, stopping them from permeating the gut and resulting in intestinal cells binding together far better.

It Can Help to Alleviate Discomfort from Arthritis

Research has shown conclusively that cannabis can reduce pain, inflammation and help to promote good sleep and this can help those who suffer from conditions like rheumatoid arthritis. Research published in 2011 explained that arthritis patients at a number of hospitals were prescribed Sativex by the rheumatology departments. Sativex as a pain reliever with a cannabinoid base. After two weeks, those on the Sativex reported that they felt less pain and slept much better compared to those who were given a placebo.

It Can Help Keep Your Weight Down and Your Metabolism Up

Research published recently said that those who smoke cannabis are significantly thinner than an average person and a much faster metabolism. They also have a better reaction to sugars, despite the fact that the cannabis causes them to get "the munchies", resulting in a higher calorie intake.

The study looked at the data form over 4500 American adults. 579 of these people were already cannabis smokers and around 2000 had used the drug at some point in the past. A further 2000 had never touched the drug. The study covered the response to eating sugar in all subjects, looking at the levels of insulin and blood sugars immediately after eating sugar and after a period of 9 hours without any food at all. The study showed that those who used or had used cannabis wee skinnier and had a healthier metabolic reaction to the sugar.

It Can Help to Improve Lupus Symptoms

Medical cannabis is now being used to help treat Systemic Lupus Erythematosus, an autoimmune disease in which the body turns on itself and starts attacking. Nobody knows the reason why this happens.

Some of the chemicals contained in cannabis calm the immune system and it is believed that this is how it can help Lupus sufferers. Added to that is the fact that we know the cannabis can deal positively with pain and nausea, making life much easier for the Lupus sufferer.

It Boosts Brain Activity

Many people have a misconceived idea that cannabis users are always stoned and mellowed out. However, research has shown the opposite to be true, that the use of cannabis can actually increase creativity and brain activity. Although many users suffer with short-term memory problem, they do excel at tests that ask them to conceive new ideas.

One of these studies requested the participants to come up with some different words that were related to a specific concept. This that were using cannabis produced a wider variety of concepts, which leads to the belief that the drug enhances the activity in the brain, thus enhancing creativity.

Other studies have showed that some users become more fluent verbally and are bale to come up with more words, perhaps those that they would not have used when not under the influence. Some of this has been attributed to the extra dopamine that is released in the brain. The dopamine reduces the inhibitions of the user and relaxes them, which gives the brain more ability to see things in a different way.

It Can Help with Crohn's Disease

Crohn's is an inflammatory disease that affects the bowel. It can cause severe pain, diarrhea, vomiting, weight loss and much more beside. Recent studies carried out in Israel have showed that using cannabis reduced the symptoms significantly in 10 out of 11 people. In 5 of the people studied, the disease went into complete remission.

That is just a very small study but it isn't the only one and others have shown the same or similar effects. The cannabinoid compounds help the gut to regulate the bacteria and to improve the function of the intestines.

It Can Help People with Parkinson's Disease

Recent studies, again carried out in Israel, show that use of cannabis can reduce the tremors and pain associated with Parkinson's Disease, as well as improving sleep. The most impressive aspect of the research was the improvement of the fine motor skills in some of the patients.

Israel has legalized medical cannabis for several different conditions and much of the research into the properties and medical benefits of the drug are carried out there, with full support of the Israeli government.

It Can Help PTSD Sufferers

Some US States have already approved the use of medical cannabis as s form of treatment for veterans who suffer with post-traumatic stress disorder and now, for the first time, the US government has actually signed off on a proposal to study the effects of the drug on the disorder. The treatment uses vaped or smoked cannabis, a form of the drug that is not classified as having any applications medicinally.

Cannabinoids that are similar to THC occur naturally in the body and they help to regulate the part of the system that causes anxiety and fear in the brain and the body.

It Can Help to Protect the Brain Following a Stroke

Research that was carried out at the University of Nottingham has shown that cannabis may be of some help in protecting the brain from stroke damage. Studies on moneys, rats and mice showed that the cannabis actually reduces the size of the brain area that is affected by the stroke.

This is not the first study to show that cannabis has neuroprotective effects. Other research on the plant show that it can also help to protect the brain after concussion or after any other traumatic event.

It Helps to Protect the Brain

There is a fair bit of research that shows this, including a study published recently that focused on mice. The research found that use of cannabis reduced the amount of bruising that occurs in the brain with concussion or a similar trauma. It also showed that the drug could help with the healing process.

Lester Grinspoon is a firm advocate of cannabis and is also a Harvard Professor Emeritus in psychiatry. He has recently sent an open letter to the commissioner of the NFL, saying that he believes the NFL should not test their players for the drug. He also said that he believed the NFL should begin to fund more research into the ability of cannabis to help protect the brain. He says that, should the medical research prove that cannabis is effective as a neuroprotective agent, he would deem it suitable for athletes to use the drug.

It Can Help Stop Nightmares

This is something of a complicated issue because cannabis can have both a positive and a negative effect. Cannabis does disturb sleep cycles because it interrupts the final REM stages of sleep in the long term, this could cause significant problems for regular users.

However, if a person suffers from very serious and threatening nightmares, especially if they also suffer from PTSD, cannabis can help. Nightmares, in fact most dreams, tends to occur in REM sleep stage and, because cannabis interrupts this, the dreams and nightmares are less likely to occur. Research has shown that, by using a synthetic version of THC, PTSD sufferers were able to report lower instances of having nightmare.

As well as this, even if regular use is bad for sleep patterns, cannabis may actually prove to be a better aid than many other substances, such as sleep medication or alcohol, which have been shown to have worse effects on the quality of sleep. However, research is ongoing at this time.

It Can Stimulate the Appetite and Reduce Chemotherapy Side Effects

This is one of the most well documented uses for medical cannabis. People who are being treated for cancer with chemotherapy suffer with terrible nausea, regular vomiting and a severe lack of appetite, not to mention the pain that goes with it. These can add to the problem by casing their own additional health problems.

Cannabis has been shown to reduce all of these side effects – helping to alleviate the pain, reducing the feelings of nausea, cutting down the number of times vomiting occurs and boosting the appetite. Many cannabinoid drugs that contain THC have been approved for use by the FDA for these purposes.

It can Help a Person to Cut Down on Alcohol

Cannabis is, without a doubt, a far safer substance than alcohol, even if it isn't without its own risks. It is nowhere near as addictive as alcohol and it doesn't cause anywhere near the amount of physical damage. Alcoholism and other similar disorders involve serve disruption to the endocannabinoid system in the body and it is for this reason that it is believed cannabis can help.

Recent research has shown that people turn to cannabis instead of alcohol or tobacco as it is less addictive the side effects are not as adverse and withdrawal symptoms are less likely to occur. There is no doubt that some people do become dependent on the drug and it must never be used as a cure for other substance abuse issues. However, it is less harmful and it can help.

Now that you know all the wonderful benefits of using cannabis, in the next chapter we are going to look at how to grow your own.

Chapter 4:
Growing Your Own Cannabis

When the weather begins to change and warm up, something seems to happen inside of many cannabis users. There seems to be something about the warmer months of the year that brings out the "toker" in many people and for some people, it brings out the green thumbs as well.

Growing cannabis is not difficult and many users prefer to turn their attention from using the drug to growing it, just one of the many facets of cannabis. With medical cannabis now being legal in many States, more and more people are asking how to go about growing their little pot of, well "pot".

How to Get Started

The first thing to know is where you can purchase the best seeds. Different seed banks are situated all over the world. For instance, there are some found in Canada, The United Kingdom, Netherlands and Spain. If you are wondering why you should purchase from these countries instead of other countries that may also sell cannabis? It's because they are more permissive about their marijuana rules as compared to other nations. These countries will give you the least amount of trouble.

Do remember that different countries in other parts of the world could seize the cannabis seeds that you may have purchased. You may even potentially face imprisonment for possession, especially if you were to do it in some parts of the United States. While some states are allowed to produce medical marijuana, attempting to purchase from the United States and then returning to your home country (if you live elsewhere) can be tricky.

How Legal are Cannabis Seeds?

Wherever you currently live, you need to consider the rules about cannabis in your country. Some territories will allow you to grow cannabis with ease, but there are also some countries that are very strict when it comes to this. In some countries, you are not allowed to grow, sell or even possess cannabis seeds, so if you are caught with seeds, you may have to spend some time in prison. In other countries, they are more lenient with their rules. Some even sell cannabis seeds as souvenirs. Just make sure that they will not be seen by the US Customs and Border Protection because they will be taken.

Methods of Harvesting

If it is your first time to try breeding cannabis, you may be surprised to know that your method of harvesting it will also have an effect on the quality of the overall of the product. The way that it is handled can change the result of a real strain. If you are too rough in handling your cannabis, there is a big chance that it will not turn out as good as you could have hoped.

Flushing

Some people tend to try flushing before they harvest the cannabis for real. Flushing is supposedly done to remove the various residues that may cause the marijuana not to taste good. Some have reported that because they have purchased cannabis that did not undergo flushing, what they have received is too bitter for their liking. Of course, it is important that a flush is completed properly, just enough to clean the cannabis well.

Harvesting Time

Did you know that one of the most important things that you have to remember when it comes to harvesting your cannabis? Is making sure it is the right time to gather the plant crop. It is important to only harvest marijuana when it is completely ripe. There may be some factors that will allow you to know if it is ripe for picking such as the following:

- The overall color of the plant particularly the pistils.

- The appearance of trichomes.

Only when the plants are indeed ripe for picking will the cannabinoids and terpenes will be able to give the full flavor and effect of the cannabis.

Trimming

It is important to remember that there will be times when you need to cut your cannabis, and if it is not done properly, there is a big chance that you will ruin the overall strain of the plant. Some of the traits that can make your cannabis unique are very fragile so manhandling your cannabis will change things tremendously for you. You do not want your plant to fall short of its full potential because of your actions, right? The best way for you to trim your buds is to cut it by hand. There is no need for the use of other machines that may promise to do the same tasks efficiently for you. Hand trimming is still the best way that you can let your plant reach its full potential without hurting it in the process.

The Process of Curing Cannabis

This does not refer to the period after the cannabis has already been harvested, this is already the end, and you can sell it. You need to make sure that you will still cure it and dry it so that it can be ready. There are times when the cannabis can change from good to extraordinary because of the curing process. Mostly what changes during the curing process is the cannabinoids will be modified to their psychoactive state.

The most common method of curing cannabis is through curing in glass jars. This method involves placing the marijuana leaves in glass jars. This method will allow you to let excess moisture be bumped off or removed from the plant leaves.

When the curing process is completed correctly, this can significantly improve the flavor of the cannabis. For instance, the grassy flavor will be removed so that it will not taste like the natural grass that may be found in people's gardens. When the cannabis is also cured for a long time, it might bring out flavors that would not have been released. Also, if you heal it properly, you can be sure that it will not become exposed to mold and mildew that might ruin your cannabis.

It is easy to compare the curing of the cannabis to a banana. When you place the banana in your home, you cannot expect that it will be ready for eating immediately. You would have to wait for it to become ripe on its own. This process is also the same with your cannabis. Unless you are going to extract its liquid, you cannot immediately expect it to be ready for smoking or for vaping.

For the indoor grower, this is an important fact because the rowing conditions indoors must mimic the conditions in nature. That means you must control the photoperiod of the plant closely and, by this, I mean that the plant has to have at least 12 hours of light every single day to make sure that the plant does not flower until it is time.

You might be wondering why you can't just let the plant flower and then take the harvest. You could do, if you wanted to but if a plant is too immature when it flowers, the harvest will not be very good. In idea conditions, a cannabis plant will need a growing period of several weeks before being allowed to flower otherwise you will be very disappointed in what you get from it.

To keep your plant growing and to bring on a good healthy plant that is properly developed, you should grow a seedling for at least four to six weeks before you induce it to flower. During these weeks, your plant needs at least 16 hours of light every day, preferably 18 to 20 to be on the safe side. To do this indoors, even if you have a warm room with a sunny window, you will need to use a lamp to make sure your plant gets the right length of photoperiod.

The Right Lighting

This is actually the most expensive part of the whole process but, having said that, you still don't need to spend a fortune. A serious cannabis grower will tend to err towards expensive specialized lighting but for the person who is only growing one plant, there are a quite a few different lights that will do the trick.

You can even find them in hardware stores at prices as low as around $25 to $30 but you will need to ensure that you have a special fixture, as they will not attach into any standard light fitting in safety – the fixtures could cost as much as $200. If you choose to go down this route, look for an HID (high intensity discharge) bulb of 250 watts, either metal halide (MH) or high pressure sodium (HPS).

If you don't want to go to that expense and you do have a good warm window, with plenty of daylight and sunlight of the most part of the day, you can use fluorescent lights to provide the necessary lighting when the sun goes down. Look for T5, T8 or

CFL fluorescent bulbs – these will give your plant sufficient light to stay in the vegetation state.

Do keep in mind that the lower the intensity of the light, the less development you will see in your plant. You should only opt for fluorescent lighting if your plant receives plenty of strong and warm light during the day. If it doesn't, the plant will start to bolt and become spindly as it looks for the light; it will certainly not develop as it should do to produce a good harvest. To be on the safe side, you should opt for the HID 250 watt bulb and keep the plant in an enclosed place where you can keep the light on it for the full period through the day.

Start the Flowering Period

When your plant has developed sufficiently and has reached a size and strength where enough flowers can be produced for a good harvest, you need to start changing the lighting cycle. Gradually begin to reduce the light period down so that the plant has 12 hours of light and 12 hours of darkness. You will still need to use your light because, during the light period, the plant is going to need a very strong light to help it produce enough energy to bear the flowers.

Even outdoor growers struggle with this sometimes, as you can't predict how much strong sunlight you will get every day.

Ensure that your plant is in an enclosed space where the light can be positioned overhead and you can have full control over the cycle. Use a standard timer on a 12-hour cycle for this.

During the dark period, your plant must be kept in total darkness – this is why a well-sealed cabinet usually works bet. Any light leaking in can cause stress to the plant, disrupt the flowering cycle and confuse the plant. This could force it to produce seeded flower (hermaphrodite) or weaken the quality and amount of harvest you eventually get.

When your plant is eventually ready for harvesting, the flowers, leaves and stems need to be completely dried out.

Tips and Tricks

Apart from making sure that your plant is grown in the right conditions, you also need to think about the type of container you are going to sue, the growing medium and feeding your plant the right nutrients.

If you are growing just one plant, you can use any type of breathable plant container, perhaps a fabric pot. It must have plenty of drainage holes and a saucer or stand to catch the run-off water. Do not let or plants sit in stagnating water for too long as it will change the pH and the growing medium and plant will eventually draw it back up again – not good for the plant. Stagnating water is also very attractive to mold and bugs.

For the medium, consider using organic potting soil, coco, peat or a sphagnum based medium. Make sure that it is airy and allows the air to get to the roots of the plant. The roots take oxygen in and the plant above the soil takes in CO2.
 Some growing mediums already contain a certain amount of organic nutrient like sea kelp or guano and this will reduce how much nutrient you need to feed the plant. The right medium can eliminate the need to feed your plant until the flowering stage. Do not use synthetic nutrients, as they are full of salt and artificial nutrients; instead lean towards organics. Synthetics can cause a lot of problems for your plant and are best avoided at all costs.

All that remains is for me to say have fun and use the experience to connect with nature. Enjoy and learn from the process and reap the best harvest you possibly can.

Chapter 5 –
How to Use Cannabis

It used to be that the only way to use cannabis was to some it but, now, users have many more options. It is very difficult to pin down the best way because everyone is different and there are new ways of consuming cannabis appearing on a regular basis. While smoking is still the most popular form, vaping is fast chasing it and more and more people are also including cannabis in their food. And that's not to mention the sprays, the oils and many other formats besides.

How you use cannabis comes down to your own personal preference and your priorities in terms of price, convenience, health, strength and other factors. In this chapter, I am going to look at some of the different ways that you can use cannabis, so that you can decide which way suits you the best.

Smoking

Smoking is not on the most popular method, it is the fastest way to get the THC into the blood. The cannabinoids get into the body via the lungs, and are then taken straight into the bloodstream.

A recent study showed that people who inhaled cannabis through smoking report that the effects took place within minutes. However, smoking it is also doing the most damage to the lungs because, not only are you taking in the drug, you are taking in other materials.

Let's look at the different options you have for inhaling cannabis:

Joint — this is the most popular method of delivery and many smokers, particularly Europeans, like to add tobacco to the cannabis to provide an extra instant high.

Blunt - this is like a joint but uses cigar papers for rolling instead of cigarette papers. A blunt is thicker and can hold more cannabis, which makes it a very powerful method of delivery.

Bowls and Pipes — This is a very quick and very easy way to consume cannabis. All you do is light it up and away you go. This method is just as effective as a blunt or a joint although, because there isn't any paper involved, the taste will be somewhat different.

Bowls have to be lit for each hit nice if you want to save some for later but not very convenient for those who are outdoors on a breezy day.

SAFETY NOTE – if you are desperate for a hit, do not make the mistake of trying the light the final amounts of resin in the bowl. The resin has a very high ratio of THC to carbon, tar and ash. Doing this can also heat the bowl extremely quickly and you may end up burning yourself.

Bongs - bongs come in all different sizes and shapes and can often look very appealing. For this reason, they can be purchased as decoration items as well as for cannabis use. The most popular form is the gravity bong. This uses gravity to push the smoke into the chamber.

Bubblers – These are small bong, small enough to carry around in a pocket. Like the bong, a bubbler gives the smoke chance to cool, meaning a user can take in more and take advantage of a bigger hit.

Dabs – Dabs are also known as Butan Hash Oil (BHO) and are extremely potent oils that should be smoked with the help of a rig. A rig is similar to a bong bowl but it has a blowtorch with it. It is an intense version of flash vaping.

Although it looks like a dangerous method, it is actually reported to be the safest and the healthiest. This is because the user only inhales the smoke, none of the plant matter. However, it is not a recommended method for beginners and has earned itself the nickname of being the "crack" of pot – you use this method entirely at your own risk.

It doesn't matter how you inhale cannabis, all of the above methods, apart from dabs, have more chemicals in them because you are burning the flower. If you don't want to get involved in smoking cannabis, there are plenty of other ways to get your hit.

Vaping

Vaping is somewhat similar to smoking but, instead of burning the cannabis, you are just heating it instead. As such, that makes vaping healthier as it gets rid of the potential to cause pain in the lungs and the throat, the same pain that you get from inhaling burned organic matter. That said, there isn't any evidence, scientific or otherwise, to prove that smoking is more detrimental to the health than vaping.

Vapes come in a variety of different sizes and shapes. Some of them are large tabletop vapes while others are smaller, more portable ones that fit neatly in a pocket. Vapes can be used with cannabis oils but, be aware that some of these oils may contain upwards of 80% THC, in comparison to around 5 to 25% for the flowers. As you would expect with a much higher concentration of THC, the effect on the body is also a good deal stronger.

Other Methods

If you are not interested in smoking or vaping cannabis, there are lots of other options for you to choose from. These days, many people put cannabis into their food, although there are other ways to take it in. No matter which method you choose, whenever you take your cannabis orally, the effect will take longer to appear and will be a good deal stronger. Many users who ingest their cannabis in this way report that it can take up to 30 minutes before the effects are felt; some say over an hour.

The peak mark for the effects is normally around two hours after ingestions and can last for upwards of 6 hours, sometimes more. The reason the effects are stronger is because, when the cannabis undergoes digestion in the body, the cannabinoids are transformed chemically, making them much stronger. On top of that, it is much harder to keep track of your dosage when you are eating it. While a dispensary is regulated, a pot brownie isn't.

Because it can take anywhere up to two hours for the full effects to be felt, it is very easy for a beginner to take in too much, and they will suffer the consequences in a big way. Oral cannabis consumption is a good method for those using medical cannabis to control pain as you don't need to take it so often. For recreational uses, it is a good choice for that long bus journey where you don't need to get up and move for a while, simply because, if you do take too much, you will fall asleep.

Let's have a look at some of the more popular oral options:

Snacks - this covers cookies, brownies, cakes, as many snack options as you want. If you cannot find the food you desire, search the internet – you will find a recipe somewhere.

Capsule – Cannabis can be taken in pill or capsule form, just like any other type of medication. This is a good option for those who don't want to smoke it but you do need to be aware that cannabis in capsule form is way more potent and highly concentrated. Be aware of the dosage you are taking.

Tinctures - Some people prefer to take their cannabis by dissolving it on their tongue. This is one of the most underrated methods and is a liquid form of the drug. It is another good method for those who do not want to smoke.

All you do is place a couple of drops on the tongue and wait for them to dissolve. The effects will ick after about five to fifteen minutes and the effect will be based on the strain of cannabis that you use.
This form of cannabis has no smell because it is an alcoholic extract and, as such, this makes it a very convenient form.

Spray – A THC spray is nothing more than a tincture in a bottle and it only take a couple of sprays to put you on the path to a high.

Drinks - Although it isn't easy, you can make cannabis tea and cannabis beer, as well as wine and coffee. It isn't the most popular way of taking cannabis but it does have the same effect.

If you are not looking for the normal high from cannabis, you do still have options. For those who are looking for a pain relief method or a way of reducing inflammation on a part of the skin, you can use cannabis topically. These are simply creams that have an infusion of cannabis in them and you just use them as you would any other cream or lotion. This method does not provide any psychoactive effect so it is the perfect option for someone who wants the medical benefits without the high.

Chapter 6:
Cannabis Extracts

Extraction has been a process that's been around for quite a long time. Even in the ancient times, extraction has been carried out to produce natural byproducts. The primary goal of removal is to make sure that the right compounds are taken, and the unhealthy compounds are to be removed. The unusable and undesirable plant material will be subsequently removed. Over the years, the methods used for extraction have also been improved.

If you search the market for cannabis extracts, you will not be disappointed because many are available.

Cannabinoids and Terpenes are the components that people usually hope to extract from marijuana.

The Basics of Cannabis Extraction

The process of the extraction of cannabis is highly different from the one that people used to do to get vitamins and minerals. Extraction has also been done in a view to removing the caffeine from coffee. In cannabis, it is cannabinoids and terpenes that are being removed. There are various reasons why these are removed such as the following:

- Fragrance

- Flavor

- Aroma

- Physical Effect

Ultimately, having all of the components mentioned above can be ideal for a final product. There are already different types of extraction methods that are completed by a lot of experts to get those that are mentioned above.

When it comes to extracting, it is about the removal of the desirable compounds. The primary goal of the extractors is to make sure that undesirable compounds will be removed. Some examples of undesirable compounds are fat and chlorophyll both of which, people do not necessarily need. Two types of extraction can be attempted:

Slow and Short Extraction

This will allow a few of the natural and essential, desirable compounds to be extracted from the undesirable compounds.

Fast and Long Extraction

More of the beneficial compounds will be extracted but at the same time, the undesirable compounds will be received as well. People who do this may have to undergo other procedures to duly remove the undesirable compounds completely.

For most individuals who complete extractions, the extraction process can last for a few hours on average around 2 - 4 hours, but there are also some extractors who choose to do extractions that last for a whole day.

The Right Extraction Method

There are two types of extraction methods that can be used. These methods are:

- Supercritical CO_2 Extraction

  Ethanol Extraction

Experts usually choose to do the Supercritical carbon dioxide extraction. This method of extraction could not be completed using simple machinery. There is a need to make use of high-end and heavy duty machines to make the extractions possible. Carbon dioxide is carried out by a supercritical liquid to make the whole extraction process doable. There is a need to increase the temperature and pressure until carbon dioxide reaches its practical form. The CO2 will then pass through an extraction vessel which is made out of finely ground cannabis grains.

While the carbon dioxide solvent passes through the finely ground cannabis grains, efficient removal will become achievable. Do remember that extraction will not be impressive if the cannabis seeds are not adequately ground.

There is a back pressure regulator that is in charge of the strength of the whole machine. At the same time, various pumps will make sure that the right amount of cannabinoids and terpenes are removed. After the required number has already been extracted, the next process is to ensure that the carbon dioxide liquid solvent is formed back into its gaseous form. Usually, after the entire process is complete a dark resin will be left behind.

Let us also not forget that there is again another method that can be carried out to extract some of the components of cannabis. This approach is called ethanol extraction. This type of extracting method is known to be the quicker method of extraction but like mentioned earlier, it does not mean that just because it is fast, it is more efficient. Since ethanol is polar by nature, it will be able to extract some of the undesirable compounds. Once all of the needed components are extracted, the extracted resin will still have to undergo other processes actually to clean it out.

The Process of Refinement for Cannabis Extractions

For the extraction process of supercritical CO_2 extractions, the method is called winterizing. This method makes sure that the purified cannabinoids and terpenes are removed from the other undesirable compounds. It will become even purer because of the whole extraction process that it will go through. Carbon filtration procedure is the type of extraction process that is completed when the ethanol process is carried out to extract the cannabinoids and terpenes from the cannabis. Carbon filtration process will make sure that chlorophyll, as well as other pigments, will be duly removed so that it will become pure and potent.

If there is a significant amount that needs to be refined, this will make the whole process even harder to execute. The reason this process becomes difficult is due to the different machines that are required to make the whole extraction process efficient. Some things that need to be monitored are the following:

- Proper maintenance

- Proper training of staff members who will oversee the entire extraction process.

- Sanitation

- Improved workflow

There are a lot of researchers who put a lot of effort into making sure that they have created the best method possible to refine efficiently the extractions that they have received from the Cannabis. The most important thing to look for with extractions is the purity of what has been extracted.

Chapter 7:
The Color of the Cannabis

Have you ever wondered why some plants are colored differently? This difference in color is mainly due to the various factors that may affect the color these can include the environment and genetics. There will be times when you will see some plants that have unique coloring which contains color combinations that are not previously believed possible. You will learn more about the different colors of the cannabis and why they have gained unique colors as you continue reading.

Genetics - How It Can Influence the Color of the Cannabis

There are genetic building blocks available, which are meant to provide plants with their vibrant color. While most of the time, the anthocyanins, which is responsible for the coloring of cannabis plant is green. It may also appear in different colors that can give marijuana their unique appearance. In case you are not aware, anthocyanins are a family of flavonoids. They can provide different color pigments to plants. The standard colors are red, blue and purple.

If you see some plants that are colored differently from the usual, you can expect that this is because of anthocyanins. There is where some cannabis will show more colors than usual, and you can expect that this will also have an effect on its overall impact as well as its scent. Some strains are aptly named because of their color, and you can expect their color to appear again and again.

There are also some cannabis plants that may have more than one color although the colors may be similar to each other. When there is more than one color present in a cannabis plant, this can indicate that the plant has high levels of anthocyanins. A lot of breeders who would like to lure people through the colors of the cannabis do go after these marijuana plants.

The Change from Green to Purple

A lot of times, cannabis plants usually start out as green. Green is usually the primary color because plants need chlorophyll to undergo photosynthesis. When marijuana matures, the chlorophyll is duly lessened, and this gives the anthocyanins to appear. That is why the color of the cannabis may change as it grows. Different environmental conditions may explain why there are differences in the production of chlorophyll.

It is safe to assume that when cannabis plants turn red, blue or purple, this indicates that they have high anthocyanin levels and if they are picked out, there is a big chance that they will also produce other seeds and later on plants that are also colorful by nature. Cannabis that does not display the colors as mentioned above may be richer in carotenoids. The color that carotenoids usually give is similar to gold.

Different Factors That Can Affect the Color of Cannabis

It has been mentioned earlier that various reasons in an environment may aptly change the color of the cannabis. Getting to know more about it will help you understand this phenomenon. It is important to remember that not all types of cannabis will suddenly display a change in color. Only those that have this in their genes will showcase the sudden change. You cannot expect the marijuana plant that you have picked out to change its color suddenly once it matures if its parent plants did not undergo a change in color too.

Temperature

One of the main triggers that can change the color of the cannabis is the change in temperature. When the temperature starts to drop, there is a possibility that some strains of the red, blue and purple will start to appear.

High pH Levels

You have to remember that there are instances when the color of the cannabis will also improve when the environment is more acidic than usual. The color of the marijuana will help determine what the current condition is. For instance:

- Red and pink coloration will be induced because of acidic environments.

- Purple coloration will be evident when the pH is neutral.

- Blue becomes apparent when the pH levels become higher than usual.

- Yellow color becomes visible throughout alkaline conditions.

It is important to remember that it does not mean that just because cannabis is in a color other than green, it is already more potent than the others. It is highly likely that some cannabis breeders will only choose colorful ones in order to catch the attention of first-time buyers who are usually attracted to different things that are also colored uniquely.

Factors that can affect the Cannabis Strain

It is evident that different marijuana strains are different for everyone. How can you possibly choose the color strain that is right for you? How can you determine the strain that you are going to produce? You can look for the following features to be able to choose right strain.

Have you ever wondered why you have a particular taste for food, perfume? Have you ever wondered why you are
not as tall as your classmate or why the color of your hair is different from other people? You already know by now that it is because of genetics although when you were younger, you have probably wondered about these things many times.

You have to remember that this is also the same with cannabis, it will be able to display some of the attributes that are similar to their parents. Breeders may also play a huge role in the traits of the cannabis that they would like to play up so that it can have a different effect on people who are going to use it. Some types of marijuana are meant to be enjoyed because of the effects that they can give while others are well known for providing some flavor that is not available in other types of cannabis.

Some strains are highly stable which means that they are potent and can give the kind of effect that you want, but there are also some that are products of experimentation so they may not be able to give what you are looking for outright. Some breeders become disappointed when the genes of the plants that they have chosen are unstable because they are left with other volatile cannabis in their very own gardens.

You can always decide if you would like to grow your strain from the seed that you may have purchased from the marketplace or may choose a clone if you are confident that the plant that you already have has a real strain. There are some cons to be remembered, however. For seeds, you would need to wait for a long time before you can see if the strain has turned out right. You would need a lot of time, patience and dedication to see if you have made the right choice. If it does work out well, then this is good but if it does not, it means that you have only wasted time. For cloning, this is beneficial because you already know what you are going to expect but remember that you cannot make use of the same plant too many times as it tends to deteriorate over time.

Environment

You have to remember that where you are going to plant your cannabis will also have an effect on how it will grow. Some breeders will choose to grow their cannabis outdoors while there are also some who would rather grow their marijuana indoors. There may be ongoing debates about this mainly because of the Breeders' different beliefs but the fact remains that the environment where the cannabis is to be planted will also have different effects on the overall outcome.

When it comes to the marijuana that is planted outdoors, these plants become exposed to nature so they naturally receive the elements that indoor plants may not get exposure to, but there will be moments in which they may get exposed to conditions which are not suitable for their growth. Indoor plants, on the other hand, can be controlled so only a limited number of elements may help make it grow to reach its full potential. Do remember that no matter what your choice is going to be in growing your cannabis, to consider that everything that you do will have an effect on how it is going to turn out.

Some factors related to the environment that may affect how your cannabis grows are the following:

Grow Techniques - some people choose to grow cannabis the natural way which means that they make use of soil in order to help their plants grow, but some people are saying now that aeroponic methods are better when it comes to making cannabis grow.

Nutrients - Plants will not be able to survive without nutrients, and the type of nutrients that cannabis plants are receiving will have an effect on the kind of strain which it will produce. The growth and potency of cannabis become different because of adopting such nutrients.

Light - If cannabis is to be exposed to natural light then this is good, but some cannabis breeders would like to make sure that they can be more in control of the lighting that the plants will receive. This is the reason why some breeders purchase a light for their plants. Controlling the amount of light that plants gets exposed to is also important. There are already some reports where some plants have gotten burnt because the light is too bright. Of course, on the other hand, some plants are also underexposed to light.

Temperature - It is already evident that when it comes to temperature, the factor of humidity will also come into play. This rule of nature means that if there is a change in temperature, there is a big chance that there will also be a change in humidity as well. While controlling the temperature is sometimes not possible especially if the cannabis is being planted outdoors, letting the marijuana become exposed to high levels of humidity might make it more susceptible to various elements that will not make it as potent as you want it to be. Sometimes, cannabis becomes exposed to different

contaminants that will make it worthless, and you would not want that.

Carbon Dioxide - It is important to know that like other plants, cannabis would need carbon dioxide to survive. In the process of photosynthesis, carbon dioxide is known to be one of the essential elements required to make it all possible. Most growers take extra care to ensure that there is sufficient carbon dioxide present in the plant growing cycle.

PH Levels - While there are times when the color of the cannabis may change because of being exposed to an acidic environment, pH levels should be neutral to ensure that the marijuana will not be exposed to various nutrient deficiencies.

Chapter 8:
Cooking with Cannabis

If you don't want to smoke or vape cannabis, or you just want the medicinal properties, the ideal way is to cook with it. The important thing is that you understand how to cook with it. Most recipes will require you to use canna oil or canna butter, used in place of normal butter or oil. If you want the psychoactive properties of the cannabis, it has to be heated and that includes when you eat it. If you try to eat the cannabis without preparing it, it will not taste too good because the human digestive system cannot digest the THC in the cannabis. THC is fat-soluble so you have to cook it with some kind of fat – oil, bitter, milk, etc.

Do It Yourself (DIY) Extraction Methods

There are a few ways to extract cannabis, from the simply DIY method to more complex methods, which really are best left to the professional. When you extract the cannabis at home, it is usually in the format of a fat that is infused with the drug. When it is heated, the THC in the cannabis binds to the fat, making a very easy method of bringing the activated cannabis into your life without having to smoke it.

Common methods include:

Canna Butter

Whether your preference is for an herbal butter or for a clarified ghee to spread on your toast for breakfast, canna butter is one of the most versatile of all the extraction methods. Here's how to make it:

Ingredients

- ¼ oz. finely ground cannabis bud

- ½ cup unsalted butter

Equipment

- Medium sized pan

- Wooden ladle

- Metal strainer

- Spoon

- Container that has a good sealing lid

Instructions

- Melt the butter gently over a low heat

- Add the finely ground bud to the butter in small amounts, stirring well to incorporate
- Simmer for about 45 minutes over a low heat, stirring often. You should start to see a few bubbles showing up on the surface of the butter

- After about 45 minutes, strain the mixture into your container, filtering the buds out with the strainer

- Use the spoon to press as much of the butter through the strainer as you can

The butter in your container should have a slight green color to it – this is the coloring from the cannabis. You can now use your canna butter to infuse your meals.

Canna Oil

Canna oil can be used in many different ways, from a salad dressing to a sauce and even in your baked goods.

Here's how to make it.

Ingredients

- 6 cups of olive or canola oil

- 1 oz. finely ground cannabis buds OR 2 oz. of dried, trimmed and ground leaf

Equipment

- Heavy bottomed saucepan or a double-boiler

- Wooden spoon

- Metal strainer

- Airtight container

Instructions

- Heat the oil slowly over a low heat for a couple of minutes – you should be able to detect the oil's aroma

- Add a little of the cannabis to the oil and stir it, making sure the cannabis is fully coated in oil

- Keep on adding it and stirring until all the cannabis is in the oil
- Simmer for about 45 minutes over a low heat, stirring frequently

- Remove from the heat after 45 minutes and leave the oil to cool

- Pour it through a strainer, using a spoon to press the mixture through the strainer to get as much oil as you possibly can

- Store the oil in an airtight container in a cool place, preferably the refrigerator for up to 2 months

Working Out Your THC Dosage

One of the biggest difficulties is working out how much to use. The last thing you want is to snack on a pot brownie that gives you a high for hours and hours. The way to work out just how potent your snacks are going to be is to measure the THC in milligrams. The optimal amount to aim for is 10 mg of THC per serving of the snack, which is 1 teaspoon of canna oil or canna butter. This is enough to give a person who only uses occasionally a decent high.

You need to know the THC content of the cannabis you are using. If you buy from a dispensary, the percentage should be listed on the packet. Strains that have 15 to 20% THC are above average and if the percentage is 21% or higher, it is considered to be a very strong strain. For the purpose of working out a dose, we will assume that the strain has 10% THC. That would mean that 1000 mg of this cannabis would have 100 mg of THC. If you were aiming for 10 mg per serving, you would get the weight of the ground marijuana in milligrams and then divide it by the size of the serving. This should give you some idea of the THC amount in each serving. If this is your first time, go for 5%.

What to Do If You Eat Too Much

If you overdo it and eat too much food that has been infused with cannabis, the experience can be very intense. You can feel extremely sick, very confused, you may find that you cannot move or talk and your coordination is likely to be badly affected. You may even have hallucinations, or feel like you are floating above your body. In short, eating too much can provide an extreme "trip". Here are a few things you can try to counteract the effects if you go overboard:

- Eat citrus fruits or squeeze the fruit and drink the juice. Go for grapefruit, lemon or oranges

- Eat some pine nuts or pistachios

- Use a pine essential oil – either inhale it or use it topically

- Use something that is high in CBD – cannabidiol

Chapter 9:
The Effect of Cannabis in General

why the Scent of the Marijuana Is Divine to the Nose

T he best way to select a pot, if you want to purchase it from a retailer, is by smelling it. By smelling, you can judge the quality of product and whether you can enjoy it to the utmost level. By smelling does not mean that you have just to get a whiff of it. Rather, you have to smell it and inhale it to see if it is effective. When you have already determined the scent of the cannabis, that is when you will decide

Some Similarities between Perfume and Pot

There are a lot of researchers who have already said that there are some things that are familiar between perfume and pot. Here are some of the similarities that would have to be enumerated:

> **Outlandish Names** - You may come across different names available in the market depending

on the type of perfume or pot that you are going to purchase. They will not be labeled very simply. You can be sure that there will be a noticeable difference with their name. Of course, some rules would need

- to be followed depending on where you are going to purchase it. In Washington, you will not be allowed to smell.

Differences in Smell - You cannot expect that all of the perfumes that you can find in the market will all feel the same. It is true that there may be some scents that will seem similar, but there are some

- that will stand out for you. You cannot expect two similarly named cannabis types to smell the same.

Confusing - You have to be prepared to be confused because you may have to spend hours in a single shop just to smell the different types that are

- available. You might even have a hard time selecting exactly which one you are going to pick.

You have to remember that any cannabis that you are going to pick is highly different. It is okay if you are going to spend a lot of hours inside the shop as long as you know the right one that you are going to pick. Most of the time, people who purchase cannabis for the first time, are surprised with what they are going to receive because what they have expected to buy is not what they buy at the end. It is important that people will only have the perfect match available.

It has been said that some types of cannabis are considered to be similar to the herbs that people may use for wellness and good health. Some are even analogous to the kinds of herbs that are being used for aromatherapy. There are some notes of the cannabis that could be considered highly similar to perfumes as well. Of course, it is not expected that people will all like the same type of marijuana. There may be some strong scents that individuals who have been taking cannabis for a long time will like, but these scents may not be favored by first timers who are searching for more mellow scents that they can appreciate.

Methods of Consumption and Preserving the Scent

When it comes to knowing how the smell of the cannabis is going to remain for a long time, the way that it is consumed will play a huge factor. The smell of the marijuana mainly comes from one of its parts, the terpenes. The terpenes are present in all flowers, and this is also in charge of giving flowers their unique smell. The terpenes in cannabis are meant to attract possible pollinators and at the same time, try to discourage enemies. There are over 100 types of terpenes that exist at present, and they are present in various types of cannabis.

The main reason why different scents are produced is mainly because of the different mixes of the terpenes with the cannabis. To enjoy the various scents of cannabis thoroughly, it is important that the cannabis will not be that exposed to the combustive material. This is the reason why a lot of people would rather vape cannabis rather than smoke them. If you have a vaping machine, you know that this will be good for you as you can clearly smell the scent of the cannabis. The smell is enjoyable at its best when you are in an enclosed room, and you can honestly appreciate the scent appropriately.

Another way to enjoy the smell of the cannabis is through the use of hash oil. The mixture oil will make the scent experience even more fulfilling because you will begin to feel things that you have never smelled before. Some have reported that it is similar to smelling an old perfume. The scent will be indeed intensified. The play of scents is highly different as well because some people state that some of the tones they pick up on from the cannabis that they choose are highly different. Of course, it is not expected that everyone will love the same scents.

What some people do is they play with the flower of the cannabis for about 10-15 minutes and smell it a bit before they vape it. By doing this, they have some idea of how it would feel like and this also enhances the smell pretty well.

The Correlation of Cannabis and Sleep

One of the main things that people usually have problems with is sleeping at night. For some, they are unable to sleep because they still have to do a lot of things, but there are also others who fail to get sleep because they are having trouble sleeping at night or sleeping disorders. Some people who used to suffer from insomnia or lack of sleep because of different reasons swear by the use of Cannabis for sleeping.

Here are a few things you may not know:

- Cannabis can usually help people sleep better than other medications that are available.

- Dried marijuana is usually considered to be more efficient than fresh ones.

- If you do not want to wake up at night because of your dreams then taking cannabis can help inhibit your dreams.

Research the proper facts on marijuana so that you will understand whether it can hinder your sleep or if it can help you sleep better.

At this point, you may already be familiar with the fact that the type of strains that you are going to choose will have different effects on you and your sleeping habits. If you would like to get high, you may want to pick out high THC and low CBD and vice versa if you just want to relax.

- For sleeping, it is recommended that you get the low THC and high CBD because this is not only meant to help you sleep better. Studies show that the use of this can also decrease feelings of being sleepy during day time.

Search for indica strains if you would like to sleep better. If you want a huge effect on your sleep, wherein you will not wake up at night no matter what you may get to experience then this is the best one for you to pick. It has been said that the reason why this is so effective for sleep is because of the terpene content of

- this type of strain. The indica strain is usually known to have more relaxing terpenes that will eventually make people sleep better.

Look for aged cannabis if you would like to become even sleepier. You have to remember that as Cannabis ages, the THC transforms into CBN. (cannabinol) The aged cannabis is said to have high sedative properties.
- Usually, old marijuana is converted into a medical herb after a few years. Again, it is more efficient for sleeping if it is dried.

Pair cannabis with other sleep aids to reach its full effect. There is no doubt that marijuana is already useful on its own, but it is important that cannabis will also be paired with other sleep aids so that it can be improved. By improvement, we mean that if cannabis
- would be mixed with other herbals such as lavender or chamomile, this can improve sleep even better.

It is already not surprising that due to the different things that cannabis can do, it will also allow you to have a better sleep at night. It means that you no longer have to lie awake at night waiting to sleep because you can expect that with the use of the cannabis, and you will be able to sleep without much effort. Isn't this what everyone would like to achieve?

- This feature of cannabis can be highly useful for people who have conditions that hinder them from sleeping at night. For faster results, it will be best to inhale

marijuana rather than taking in cannabis-infused edibles.

Having hangovers can be possible if you make use of marijuana so do not expect that in the morning, you are going to wake up like as if nothing has happened. The hangovers that you are going to experience will not be like the type of illnesses that you get when you drink alcohol so do not expect this kind of hangover. Rather, you will just feel a little bit light-headed. Do remember that your chances of having a hangover can be greater if you are to choose to smoke a second-grade cannabis the night before. The best way to fight the illness that you might get is by hydrating yourself and making sure that you take in some vitamins too. You will be missing out on dreaming when you take in cannabis. For some people, this may be a good thing especially if they are having a lot of unpleasant dreams lately but there may be some individuals who do not like this fact because they look forward to having dreams at night. Do remember that some reports show that when you do stop taking cannabis, you may experience more REM than usual which means that you are going to have more dreams that are more vivid and may seem more real than usual. Of course, these are just dreams, and once the need for cannabis wears off, your thoughts will return to normal.

Cannabis can be useful for people who are having trouble sleeping because of their breathing problems. For instance, there are some people with Sleep Apnea, who are unable to sleep well because their breathing may stop for a few seconds to a few minutes. It means that individuals with this condition wake up throughout the night because of the unpleasant experiences that they may be beginning to feel. It has been reported through a study that the use of cannabis may promote better breathing so that people with certain conditions will be able to avoid the harmful effects of not being able to sleep at night.

When cannabis is stopped suddenly, people will have a harder time sleeping at night. If you have always taken cannabis to help you sleep at night, and then suddenly you stop doing it, the effects may encourage you to use it again. There are certain things that you may experience at night such as the following:

1. Tossing and turning throughout the night

2. Feeling groggy and sleepy the next day brought by the lack of sleep

3. Shorter REM cycles

4. Experiencing more sleep disruptions than usual

The thing to consider here is either you do not start with taking cannabis to go to sleep at all or you are willing to take marijuana for as long as you possibly can so that you can always sleep better.

If you are to start using cannabis at an early age, there is a big chance that you will encounter more sleeping problems than the usual. You would have to be older than 15 before you are allowed to take cannabis for sleeping and some would even recommend taking cannabis when you are even much older than that.

Of course, there is still not enough evidence to cement this as a fact, but the chances are greater that there is a correlation between taking cannabis at a young age and the lack of sleep that they get to experience when they grow older.

Cannabis - A Cause of Paranoia and Anxiety

If you have taken cannabis multiple times before, you may have had different experiences with it. You are probably aware of whether the cannabis that you are taking is a good grade or if it is not good enough for you. It is also likely that you have various experiences with it that you may only consider to be bad or good.

There are already some reports of people taking in too much cannabis and as a result have experienced an episode of paranoia. There will be moments when the episode is not too bad with just worrying about the most trivial things that do not matter. There are also times when the paranoid episode is so bad that you do not want to move at all in fear that you will die although, in reality, there is nothing harmful that is going to happen to you. There are a lot of cases wherein people would have to be taken to hospitals because of extreme paranoia.

It is in great contrast to the fact that individuals who exhibit symptoms of paranoia are treated with a little bit of cannabis because this is known to decrease the anxiety that they are feeling. There are also some people who have reported that because of marijuana, they are also able to reduce their stress levels. With these conflicting stories, which should you believe in?

Both statements are correct. When people take in too much marijuana, then they may become paranoid while those who are already feeling paranoid because of different reasons may use pot to feel better about themselves. It is all about the mix of cannabis with people's brain chemistry.

Brain Chemistry and Marijuana

It is important to take note that when it comes to paranoid episodes, most of the time; it is all in people's heads. The THC strains in marijuana usually balk near the brain receptors, particularly towards the amygdala. Since the amygdala is in charge of the various responses that people may have towards certain situations, the use of marijuana can stop those thought processes. Sometimes, this is for the better, but there are also times when this can be for the worse.

For those who are not used to taking cannabis or those who have taken too much cannabis, the effect may be over excitement. The possibility that people will become paranoid because of this is great. Aside from the cannabinoids that come from cannabis, the brain also becomes filled with endocannabinoids. Endocannabinoids are compounds, and they are produced naturally by the body. Having too little of this can be bad though because it means that the brain is experiencing a lot of stress which explains why some people tend to become paranoid after taking in marijuana. Some have stated that breathing in marijuana can also affect moods because of the natural compounds that are produced in the brain after the intake.

Cannabis Affecting Pre-Existing Anxiety

There is a study created in the year 2009 which states that people who have been exposed to taking marijuana for quite a long time are said to display higher levels of stress and anxiety as compared to those who have never used marijuana or those who have not taken cannabis often.

People do become dependent on marijuana, as they do experience some level of anxiety. Most of the time, since they know that their exposure to marijuana will help stop their symptoms, this is exactly what they are doing. It means that people who take cannabis believe that it is marijuana that is helping them overcome their anxiety rather than marijuana causing their anxiety in the first place.

Some factors would have to be considered before taking in marijuana for anxiety such as the following:

- Genetic vulnerability

- Gender

- Anxiety Levels

- Personality

- Abstinence from Marijuana

Usually, those who are considered to be weaker because they are more prone to becoming addicted to marijuana are not recommended to take it as a form of medication for their anxiety, but it seems that people are ignoring this warning and are still taking marijuana for their various conditions. Some factors may pose risks such as the following:

- High Dosages

- Frequency of use

- High Amount of Cannabinoids

- Place Where Cannabis is taken

It is important to remember that for people who are vulnerable without their marijuana which they consider to be medicinal, will be unable to take it to other places that think marijuana as dangerous for the health.

It is important to take note that those who already have anxiety before they have taken marijuana show a decrease in their anxiety levels after taking it while those who never had anxiety before bearing in marijuana have shown an apparent increase in their anxiety levels after taking it. The higher the doses of THC found in the marijuana, the greater chance of experiencing anxiety too.

If you have never taken marijuana before, and you are wondering how it can affect you, it would have to depend on the factors that are mentioned above. You will not know what you are going to experience unless you are already taking it. Just acknowledging this fact may or may not increase the risk depending on how you choose to look at it.

How to Avoid Experiencing Paranoia Because of Taking Cannabis

If you are determined to try marijuana and experience its real effects, you need to make sure that you can choose the right grade and kind to ensure that it will not be too much of a problem. You can reduce the possibility of acquiring paranoia with taking in cannabis if you would consider the following:

You may choose to have cannabis that is high in CBD and low in THC to lessen the possible anxiety effect that you may begin to experience. You can be sure that you will be calmer when you choose this type of marijuana.

Do not take in too much; you may be able to control the dose when you are smoking or vaping it. Being in a place where you are comfortable will allow you to enjoy truly the whole experience. If you are going to do it in a place where you do not know anyone or are uncomfortable, you may already be anxious and paranoid to begin with.

Choose the right strain of cannabis for you. This does not mean that just because an individual strain is perfect for someone, it will already be perfect for you, you have to think carefully about it and make sure that you will do the right thing.

Chapter 10:
Precautions and Advice

You may have come across cannabis-infused edibles before without knowing how effective it is or how much you should take in. Since in some places, the edibles have already been legalized, some are also standardized to give people an even better idea about what they need. It is already a well known fact that cannabis is being used for medical and recreational purposes, and this is the reason why more and more people are finding out details themselves on how they can enjoy their cannabis edibles safely.

There are some brands like EdiPure that are already being sold in some legal markets, and they come with proper instructions like restrictions on how much should be taken. It will be up to you to follow the required dosages so that you will not go and surpass the limit.

If you have purchased EdiPure's edible products such as the cannabis infused pineapple bites or the raspberry jellies, you may already be feeling confused with the amount that you can eat without damaging your health. It is normal to worry if it is your first time. You will need to have a handy step-by-step guide so that you can have a better understanding about the dosage that you need to take with the edibles each time. You do not want to drive yourself all the way to the hospital just because you consumed too many of the edibles.

Read the Instructions Carefully

There is a good reason why there are dosing guidelines available on the back portion of the package. Things have changed, and improvements have been made since the time in which people would have to guess show much they need to take each time. The guidelines may usually start with 10 milligrams, but if you believe that you cannot take that, you may want to take only half of the recommended 10 milligrams. It means that if a bottle of watermelon slices has 10 milligrams each. You may choose to eat half of that just to start of with, or you may eat just one. Eating
more than one may change the purpose of taking it already. Do remember that there are other products created by EdiPure that have less than 10 milligrams per piece.

Know How Much You Can Tolerate

You may know yourself better than anyone else, so understand your limits well. If it is your first time, you may start by just trying half or even just one. Once you become more used to them, and you know how many you can take each time, you may start taking up to 3 milligrams. Some may be able to take more than that because they are more experienced in taking in these products. Make sure that you take note of your tolerance precisely so that this will not become a problem for you.

Patience will help you a lot

There is a big chance that you would like the effect to be fast especially after consuming the cannabis infused product of your choice, but you need to be patient because the effect might come that quickly. Remember that even if it tastes good, you need to practice restraint too because it is not the same with the other food that you love snacking on. If you eat more than you should, there is a big chance that it will prove to be too much for you. Make sure that you will take in the product one at a time so that you will know how much you are going to take.

There are different reasons why the edibles may not work immediately. You first have to consider your height and your weight. Some people will get to feel the edibles work quickly while there are also some that would have to wait for an hour before they feel the effects. Sometimes, you may need to wait for as long as two hours before you can decide if you would need to pop another product in your mouth.

Consider How Much You Have Eaten Beforehand

The contents of your stomach will also play a huge part in how fast the effect is going to be. If you have not eaten that much or if you have not even drunk anything that day, then the effects are going to be much faster. If you have not eaten anything yet, it might be best if you could start with small doses of the edibles so you can be sure you're not taking in too much. If you have just consumed alcohol, this might not be too good for you so try to limit your intake of cannabis edibles.

Find a Place Where You Can Be Comfortable

You have to remember that you do not know what the effects are going to be. The edibles might be easy to take anywhere, but you have to make sure that you will be in a place where you can be comfortable. If you want to take a large dose, it will be best if you can consume that at home. If you just want to take in single doses, then you may be able to do it when you are out. In that case that it is your first time to enjoy the product, it will be best if you are with someone else so that they can keep track of how much you have consumed so far.

Remember that the moment the edibles have taken effect, you will be transported to a level where you can feel blissful and relaxed. It will always be best that you can make it in a place where you know that nothing will harm you so that you can fully enjoy its effects without the possibility of harming yourself.

These things as mentioned earlier are the various facts that you need to know about cannabis.

Conclusion

I want to thank you for downloading my book. I worked hard to hopefully give you a lot of new information about cannabis. My goal was to give you ideas that you can actually take home and use. You should really have a good handle on what cannabis is and how to grow it. Of course, you now also know how to consume and benefit from it as well. I hope you can see that cannabis is not the dangerous drug that it is made out to be. Yes, it can be addicting, but so can tobacco, alcohol, even chocolate. The benefits far outweigh downsides and there is so much that using cannabis can help you with.

There is a reason that cannabis has been in use for so any thousands of years – because it works. The benefits are more than proven through years of research and the sooner they are more widely accepted, the sooner cannabis can be downgraded from its status as a Class 1 drug.

Hopefully, you have learned a lot about cannabis from growing it to indulging in it. Remember that moderation is always the key to enjoying marijuana. When trying to breed it, pay attention to the processes that are mentioned above to get the best strain of cannabis possible.

Hydroponics

Introduction

Hydroponics is the method of growing plants without soil by supplying them with a constant nutrient solution. Despite the fact that this method remains fairly unknown outside of a small sector of the horticultural world it has in fact been around for a long time. It is a system that was used extensively in the hanging gardens of Babylon and has been studied extensively by scientists and horticulturists for the last several hundred years.

There are many powerful reasons for commercial food growers to use this method but it is also now being used more frequently by the domestic gardener keen to produce a high yield in a small amount of space. Though it is seen primarily as a way of producing crops for the table it is also a method that can be used for the production of ornamental plants.

All plants require air, light, and dissolved nutrients to grow. Hydroponics allows for a very precisely controlled amount of nutrients, dissolved in water, to be administered directly to the root system, as the plant requires it. Because the root system is no longer obliged to spread so far in order to attain the nutrients it requires this in turn enables the grower to plant his crops at much higher densities which is just one reason why hydroponic crop yields are so much greater than the more traditional soil planted yields.

There are a variety of variations on the hydroponic theme and this book will take a look at the main options the gardener has available to them. Though some of the methods might sound overly complicated for the home gardener I advise you to persist because what at first might appear a difficult system to reproduce is in fact surprisingly easy in many cases and the increase in yields will be staggering. You have been given a great deal of information on the different types of systems that have been used often by numerous people. You have been given a detailed
description on how to construct, maintain and care for each of these systems.

Since you are a beginner, there is a possibility that you may make a mistake. It is OK to make a mistake since failures are the stepping-stones to success. Keep forging ahead! I hope you enjoy the book.

Chapter 1:

A Little History and Some Basic Principals

Primitive forms of hydroponics have been carried on by various societies for thousands of years. The word hydroponic itself stems from an amalgamation of two Ancient Greek words, 'hydro' for water and 'ponic' for work. In other words, the water was supposed to do the work that had created such toil for mankind ever since he began to practice agriculture.

Various forms of it have been carried on in Kashmir for centuries and one group, the Aztecs of America, developed a form of floating garden. Pushed to the marshy regions of Lake Tenochtitlan, in what is now Mexico, by other more aggressive tribes these nomadic people were forced to come up with a viable agricultural system in order to survive. They developed a system of floating rafts woven together out of reeds that eventually turned in to an archipelago of floating islands. These islands teemed with vegetables, flowers and even trees. The historian William Prescott recorded the destruction of the Aztec empire by the colonizing Spaniards and he described the floating gardens as 'Wondering islands of Verdure, teeming with flowers and vegetables and moving like rafts on the water.'

Many historians believe that hydroponics was an important ingredient in the creation of the famous hanging gardens of Babylon, which was one of the seven wonders of the Ancient World. If that is the case this is probably the first example of hydroponics being used as a farming method.

In more modern times the first scientific studies took place in the 1600s when the Belgian Jan van Helmont demonstrated that you could grow a willow in a tube containing 200 pounds of dried soil and fed only with rainwater. After five years the willow shoot had obtained a weight of 160 pounds whilst the soil had only decreased in weight by two ounces. He concluded that plants obtain what they require for growth from water. Whilst partially correct in his assumptions, that early demonstration failed to take into account the need for carbon dioxide and oxygen, which are also crucial to plant development.

In 1699 John Woodwards took the experiment a stage further when he grew plants in water, which contained differing amounts of diluted soil. The plants that had the highest concentrates of soil grew best. In this early version of the manmade hydroponic solution Woodwards realized that soil probably contained some nutrient crucial to plant growth but with chemistry not yet discovered he was unable to identify what those nutrients were.

Science began to gather momentum in the decades that followed and scientist were able to prove that plants absorbed water via their roots and that this then passed through their systems to be released through pores in the leaves. They also discovered that the roots also draw up nutrients and oxygen and that leaves draw carbon dioxide from the air.

In 1851 French scientist Jean Baptist Boussingault began experimenting with inert growing media and water with various combinations of elements available in soil. In 1860 the first nutrient solution in which plants could be grown was published by Professor Julius von Sachs. Various solutions continued to be developed but at this stage all studies had been based around laboratory research. It was not until the 1920's that Doctor William Gericke began to extend lab work to include outdoor crop production. In the process he termed the use of the word hydroponics and laid the groundwork for all forms of modern day hydroponics, as we know it. Developments continued of course, and still today this is an evolving science but we now have a far better handle on the methodology of growing plants without the use of soil.

There are several major benefits to using this method to cultivate plants. We immediately eliminate soil borne pests and diseases. Greater control over the plants provides more consistent size and production. Water waste is massively reduced since the water is reused. Crops mature more rapidly often allowing for two crops per year where only one is possible in traditional soil growing systems and finally greater yields are produced. In a world with decreasing natural resources and a rapidly increasing population growth it is almost inevitable that this will be an area of agricultural production that sees massive growth.

Gericke had proved that it was not soil that plants needed, it was the nutrients and moisture that the soil contained along with adequate plant support. This could be provided just as, and possibly even more effectively, by adding the exact nutrient requirements to the water and then growing the plant in an inert medium purely for stability and support. In the soil nutrients tend to be leached away from the plant roots thus forcing the plant to continuously extend its root system in an effort to reach them. Nutrients can be replaced but it is difficult to estimate the exact requirements a plant has in a system where the leaching cannot be controlled or measured accurately. This creates a further disadvantage in that the plant must waste valuable energy in root production that could be diverted to crop production. When growing in soil, the root system draws up nutrients and acts as an as an anchor and support for the plant. Provided the plant is given plenty of nutrients then the root system can be considerably smaller and the anchorage function can take place in any non-leaching material. Some hydroponic systems do away with the planting medium altogether and suspend the plant, feeding the trailing roots by a mist system. This method is perfectly successful.

Gericke's initial systems soon proved too technical for most would be hydroponic growers. One of the main problems lay in keeping a consistent supply of oxygen in the nutrient solution. Interest in the methods he developed had been triggered, however, and since then ongoing developments have made hydroponics more and simpler. Now there are huge greenhouse producers throughout the world producing very high yields. There are now over 1000 000 soil-less household units in the USA. The need to develop this system is demonstrated by these figures: in 1950 there were 3.7 million acres of land being cultivated and a population of just under 151 000 000 people. Today that population has soared to 204 000 000 and the amount of land under cultivation dropped to 3.2 million acres. With figures like this it becomes apparent that the need for viable crop production to increase and it is likely that there will be less land available for it to increase in.

Rooftops are one area that are being looked at and utilized more and more. Vast flat surfaces within city confines offer a perfect place to produce crops. What is more when we start to produce crops within urban environments we dramatically reduce the amount of mileage that the crops must travel in order to get to the end user with knock on benefits, both in terms of pollution created and freshness of the end product.

Modern hydroponics can go even smaller scale than that though. Nowadays it is easy for a homeowner to set up his own hydroponic garden in the back yard and there are even smaller units being designed for kitchens and apartments. The main requirements of water and electricity are already in place in these situations. At its most basic level here is what you will need to make your own unit.

A growing chamber or tray. This will contain the growing medium and plant roots and can be anything that holds water and is big enough for the plants you want to grow.

A reservoir. This will contain the water and nutrient system that will then be pumped to the growing chamber in a cyclical action. Once again, it can be made of just about anything as long as it holds sufficient liquid. It should, however, be light proof so as to inhibit the growth of algae and microorganisms.

A submersible pump. This does not need to be expensive and pumps the water from the reservoir to the growing chamber and back again. Fishpond pumps are often used.

Some method of delivery. This is just a system to convey the solution from the reservoir to the chamber. PVC tubing works perfectly well.

Already you have the basis for a basic but functional system. A timer is one addition that would make your life easier and costs very little. This will switch the pump on and off and ensure that the roots of the plant are always kept moist. An air pump, even one as simple as you see in small fish tanks, will help keep the solution oxygenated which is essential to plant growth and will also ensure the nutrients circulating evenly. The air pump is normally situated in the reservoir. Remember that roots need to be kept in the dark to perform at their best so depending on what growing medium you use it may be necessary to cover them in some way.

Grow lights are another addition that will give you greater control and increase the optimum growing period but these are not necessary in the most basic units. If you do opt for grow lights you may want to consider an additional timer for those.

This very basic system can be made at home or purchased as a premade kit. There are even examples of people making a system by stringing plastic soda bottles across an apartment window then linking them with PVC tubing and pumping the nutrient solution around with very good results.

The point I am trying to make is that this method of plant production is no longer restricted solely to large-scale professional outfits. There is little point in growing your own vegetables if your startup cost is such that each tomato you produce owes you twenty dollars.

Chapter 2:

Facts About the Hydroponic System

You have been told a little about the history of the hydroponics system. Let us try to learn a little more about the hydroponic system. The systems uses water as its base, but before we go into the intricate details of the system, let us try to understand why you need to use water instead of another solvent. Imagine if the earth has absolutely no water on it. Do you think you would have been able to survive on such a planet? Would there be a way for you to quench your thirst? There are numerous probes being run into finding water on other planets when there is enough water on our planet.

Every organism right from a tiny organism to a large organism always looks for water. This is because of the fact that the organisms crave for water since they have always been around water. Well, the book has a lot of information about water! You will be able to learn about the different ways you can use the sources of water around you instead of having to waste the source. When you use these sources of water along with the nutrient powders, you will find your plants extremely well in your very own garden.

You have to remember that water and fire never work together at all, but they work tremendously well when it comes to plants. If there is a forest that has been burnt down or even a tree has been burnt down, the wood turns to ash. This ash contains lot of potassium, which is an extremely important mineral for the growth of the plants. Once the water touches this ash, you will find that the potassium from the ash moves into the soil and is absorbed by the roots of the plants. Any other leaves or branches that have been decayed will be decomposed by microorganisms. The microorganisms also excrete the organic waste after consuming the dead leaves and branches. This waste also contains a lot of minerals that the plants crave for. The water helps in converting these minerals into their diluted forms that would make it easier for the plants to absorb the minerals.

If you were trying to identify the different ways you would be able to make certain that the plants in your hydroponic system have been able to obtain all the minerals they need. If this happens, you will be able to ensure that the elements in nature are able to live in perfect harmony with each other. The forests and the trees need to burn in order to ensure that the microorganisms and other insects eat well. This would mean that the monsoon would need to wash away all the nutrients from the organic waste and the minerals from the ash. This is a system that you would never find anywhere except for the rainforest.

Hydroponic systems are the perfect rainforest in your backyard! They work towards enriching the water in the system with numerous nutrients and salts that are needed in the nature. What you will need to do is create a solution that would provide all the plants with an extremely balanced system. Over the course of this book, you will learn that a hydroponic system contains a solution that is in abundance with the nutrients. The system always helps in protecting these solutions from being turned into vapor! It is for this very reason that you will be able to manage the sources of water in areas that are barren and arid. The system has often been called 'Earth Friendly gardening' and has gained immense popularity over the last few decades.

The hydroponic system is a form of art that is often called water gardening. It is always good to understand the water you will be using in this system better. You will need to know what the contents in the water you will be using. Make sure that you approach a company to understand and analyze every minute detail in the sample of water. If you know the source of the water, you will find it easier to understand and analyze the sample. What is of most importance is that you understand the hardness or the softness of the water you will be using. If the water is found to be very hard, you will find that the water has a high concentration of calcium carbonate. If the water is soft, you will find that the water is in its purest forms. Distilled water or even water that has been cured through osmosis is also in its purest form. You could use a particular nutrient solution if you need but make sure that you know whether or not the water is hard or soft. Also keep these points in mind when you are trying to purchase a set of nutrients for your solution.

You need to make sure that you do remember that it is plants you are working with. You have to also learn that the plants always absorb the nutrients that they need through their roots. Make sure that you always pay attention to the roots and do not cover them too much with the water. You have to ensure that you always keep in mind that your plants need a lot of oxygen and this is obtained through the roots.

If you are looking at keeping the roots healthy, you will need to ensure that the water always circulates well throughout the system. Make sure that the water is not stagnated since that would kill all your plants. The best part of the system is that you can grow plants of any kind without having to worry too much about the climatic conditions. All you need to do is to ensure that you have the perfect protection and the perfect solutions that are in your hydroponic system. This will ensure that you have an extremely good yield!

Chapter 3:

Hydroponics – A Quick Overview

The hydroponics system is a wonder in modern science! You have to realize that the hydroponics system always tends to have a great yield of fruits, vegetables, flowers, grains, herbs and many other plants too. You may be able to cultivate food you would never have been able to before. The system works wonders when it comes to producing food that is extremely healthy and strong. The food also has a large amount of nutrients which when consumed would leave a human being with immense energy and strength.

The newest techniques of hydroponic systems always help in providing a world with a huge quantity of food that could never be cultivated anywhere else. It has been seen that the cultivation of crops using hydroponics is extremely effective. It is for this reason that NASA has decided to cultivate crops using this system on certain planets. Only when scientists decided to understand the composition of the nutrients in plants did they understand the science behind the system of hydroponics. You may be surprised to learn the fact that these experiments have been conducted since 1600AD! The records all have the conclusions that the plants have a chance to grow up in a mixture of sand and gravel. The plants do not need soil to grow too! You could use the hanging gardens of Babylon and the floating gardens of the Aztec as classic examples. There are certain parts of Egypt that used the hydroponics systems to cultivate fruits and vegetables.

The year 1936 saw a new word – hydroponics – that was introduced by Dr. W. F. Gericke. This was the word used by him since he described a newer technique of cultivating plants. He had said that plants – various kinds of plants – could be cultivated just in water and nutrients. You will learn a little later about how this word is an apt description of the new art of gardening – hydroponic gardening.

You have been told that the hydroponics gardening method only uses a nutrient solution that will help in keeping the plants healthy and strong. The solutions that are used in this system always surround the roots and help the plant absorb the minerals and vitamins they will need using the forces of gravity. Some of the hydroponic systems use electric pumps while there are others that have the simplest working technique. Any kind of system ensures that the roots of the plants always stay in the nutrient solution that is in the reservoir. It is always good to make sure that the nutrient solution does not stagnate since that would mean the death of your plants!

You will learn that the plants that have been growing in the hydroponics system are in fact strong and healthy when compared with the plants that have been grown using traditional methods. This is because of the fact that the nutrient solution always gives your plants the balanced diet that they need. The system also keeps the plants away from any kind of pest. The systems always help in conserving and managing the sources of water around you. You will also be able to ensure that the water never goes to waste or evaporates when it is used in the system.

If the area you live in is arid or barren, you have to try to look for different ways in which you can grow your crops and hydroponic systems are one of those ways. The hydroponic system always provides your crops with water and the nutrients that your plants will need. Make sure that you grow all the plants together to ensure that you conserve a lot of space too. When the environment you grow your plants in is really clean, you will be able to ensure that the crops are being grown under ideal conditions. You will also be able to save a large amount of money. The best part is that you do not have to go looking for the right soil or even spend any money on the fertilizers and pesticides to increase the yield of the plants.

When you use the conventional methods of farming, you will be able to save immense levels of energy. Your plants would definitely be less healthy when compared to plants that have been cultivated in a hydroponics system. This is because of the fact that the hydroponic system has a lot of nutrients and minerals that the plants need. These minerals are absorbed by the roots of the plants in the system that would ensure that the plants become very healthy and strong.

Plants that have grown in the hydroponic system are always healthier than the ones that have been grown in soil. They always have a lot of energy and health since they always obtain a balanced diet of minerals and vitamins that they will need desperately. The plants are extremely strong during the worst of the climatic conditions too. I hope you have gathered a fair idea on what the hydroponics system is all about. Let us now try to understand the medium you will need to use in the system.

Understanding the growing medium

You have been told numerous times earlier that you need an extremely proper medium to grow your plants since the medium is extremely important for you to obtain a good yield. You could use either a solid or a liquid medium but either should have a set of characteristics that are listed below:

1. The particles of the medium should never be smaller than 2 millimeters. The particles should be between the sizes of 2 – 7 millimeters.

2. The medium should never decompose easily.
3. Make sure that the medium is adept at removing any excess liquid that is in the system while trying to ensure that you maintain the moisture of the plants.
4. Try to ensure that the medium is portable.
5. The medium should be found anywhere – implying that it needs to be readily available!
6. Make sure that the medium always keeps toxic microorganisms away from the humans.
7. Make sure that the medium has not been contaminated or spoilt due to the industrial wastes.

The list given below has the recommended media that you could use!

- ✓ 80 percent rice hill: 20 percent saw dust

- ✓ 60 percent rice hull: 40 percent sand

- ✓ Clean river water

- ✓ 60 percent rice hull: 40 percent ground clay bricks

- ✓ 50 percent rice hull: 50 percent ground volcanic stones

If you have decided to use the rice hulls, you have to ensure that you wash them well and keep them wet for a minimum of ten days to ensure that the seeds begin to germinate. You have to ensure that these seeds are removed once they have germinated. If you are using sawdust, you have to be extremely careful since there is a possibility that the sawdust may harm the plants. Ensure that you choose the right sawdust. You are given a better idea about the different growing media in the next chapter. Make sure that you use the ones that have been given in the chapter only!

Chapter 4:

Different Growing Mediums

There are many different growing mediums which gardeners and horticulturists all get into the habit of blending to their own requirements so here we shall look at some of the most popular and discuss their advantages and disadvantages. In all cases you are looking for a medium that is light soilless and does not contain nutrients or chemicals that will affect the plant in any way or interfere with the nutrient mix that you are providing. It also needs to be porous enough to facilitate the easy transfer of oxygen and nutrients to the roots. We use these inert planting mediums for two main reasons. They minimize the amount of light reaching the root ball and they provide a support for the plant to grow in.

Probably the three favorite materials that you are likely to come across are coconut coir, perlite and LECA.

Coconut coir

Coconut coir is a byproduct of the coconut industry. It is made of the hairy outer coating that surrounds the coconut shell and prior to being discovered as a useful product for the horticultural trade it was used for little more than stuffing for cheap mattresses. The recognition that the harvesting of peat was causing major environmental problems meant that environmentally concerned growers needed to look for new products to replace peat as a growing medium and coconut coir fitted the bill in many instances. It is sold in blocks and may also be called palm peat or simply coir.

The blocks swell to between six and eight times their compressed size when mixed with water so if you are ordering some don't be too disappointed when they arrive and appear a little smaller than you had hoped. They are particularly good at holding moisture and can absorb up to eight times their own weight. One of the disadvantages of this medium is that because it is so light it has a tendency to be washed about and for this reason is not suitable for ebb and flow systems unless combined with one of the other materials available. Growing mediums can be washed and reused after each crop. The medium is rinsed in diluted bleach then rinsed again and allowed to dry. With coir this system can only be used three or four times before it begins to break down.

Perlite

This is another product that has been around in the horticultural industry for many years. It is made by heating silica flakes that expands into very small and light pieces. These have good moisture retention and are chemically neutral so are favored by makers of potting mixes as it increases moisture holding capacity without adding weight. If cleaned by washing with bleach it can be used many times as a hydroponic planting medium. Its lightweight makes it impossible to use in the ebb and flow system unless combined with something like LECA. It has a good wicking action that makes it one of the favorite choices in wicking systems.

LECA

LECA stands for light expanded clay aggregate and is made by lightly heating clay particles until they expand from anything between six to eighteen millimeters in diameter. It is a lightweight free draining product that is very popular in the indoor plant industry and which you have probably seen used as a mulch on potted plants in shopping centers or offices. It is fairly good at holding moisture but is not on a par with something like coir in this respect and when high water retention is required the two products are often mixed at a fifty - fifty ration. The coir then holds the moisture while the LECA acts as a stabilizer to stop the coir being washed away. In this way you can get the best use from both products. You may decide to experiment on the ratios that work best for you.

These are three of the products you are most likely to come across but there are many others that will work well and you may decide to adapt to one of the products below either because of price or availability.

Vermiculite

A product with many similarities to perlite it looks like mica. It is mined in South Africa, China, Brazil and Zimbabwe. Once mined, the product is expanded by heating in a kiln and becomes very light and water retentive. Like perlite it is often used as a moisture retainer when mixed with potting composts because of it neutral pH and its lightweight. In the hydroponic arena it should be used in its pure form and not mixed with compost or soil. It does not break down and can be reused if correctly cleaned.

Peat Based Soilless Compost

Peat is mad from compressed moss and plant products that have been compressed in the ground for hundreds and even thousands of years. It has been the mainstay of the nursery industry for a very long time but its widespread use has led to a breakdown of much of the local flora and fauna in the associated environments where it is dug and there are now growing calls for its extraction to be banned in favor of more sustainable products such as coir. That said it is an extremely versatile growing medium though if you choose to use it please make sure you get it from a sustainably managed producer.

It has excellent moisture retentive characteristics and is very lightweight. Suppliers often mix it with biofungicides, which are naturally occurring anti-fungal agents, or mycorrhizae that are natural root stimulants.

Rock Wool

Suitable for both ebb and flow and for continuous drip systems rock wool is a versatile growing medium. It retains water well and its porous texture means that it facilitates the free flow of air. It is made from a type of rock that is melted and then spun to produce a material similar to foam. Two factors do need to be borne in mind when choosing this material for your growing medium. Initially it must be soaked overnight to ensure the pH is neutral and secondly it does not break down so disposal can be a problem.

Oasis cubes

This lightweight foam has been used by the florist industry for decades and is ideal for the small-scale hydroponic producer. It can hold up to forty times its own weight in water and still remain breathable. It is ideal for starting both seeds and cuttings and is very workable making it a good product for the simple wick system. These properties can be used in any of the six main growing systems and the pH is neutral.

Other options

So long as the growing medium contains no nutrients and is free draining there are plenty of products that are not related to the horticultural industry that serve well in the hydroponic world and you are free to think out of the box and experiment with whatever ingredients you find that may fit the bill. Those lightweight packaging peanuts you had sitting around in the garage with no real use for, are one example. Builder's sand was used widely in the early days of hydroponics. It needs to be rinsed to leach out any chemicals and it has a low water retention capacity but it does work. Be careful though because it tends to pack down when it has been wet a few times and then drainage will deteriorate.

Gravel is another cheap and easy to find material. It offers no water retention but sometimes both of these qualities might prove desirable. In Australia sawdust is often used for large-scale tomato growing because it retains moisture and is often free. If you decide to experiment with this material make sure it has not been polluted with any products whilst still at the sawmill. They could damage your plants. It does tend to break down but as it is usually free it is easily replaced.

Rice hulls are a bi product of rice farming. They are as effective as perlite though they do decompose so will have a limited life span. As it is usually cheap or free this may not be an issue and regular replacement is recommended, as there tends to be a buildup of salts that are detrimental to plant growth.

What I hope I have demonstrated is that there is no specific product you have to use provided it is pH neutral and drains well. I have heard of instances of people using torn up cardboard, broken brick and tiles and even the stuffing out of an old mattress. Feel free to experiment with whatever comes to hand.

Chapter 5:

The Different Hydroponic Systems

A lthough there is a great deal of variety in the different types of hydroponic systems in essence it comes down to six different types. The drip system, the ebb and flow system, N.F.T., the water culture system, Aeroponics and the wick system. These systems can all be modified to suit the environment and budget of the individual user and the space they have available to them. In choosing an appropriate system for your own needs you need to consider these things as well as the size and types of plant you will be growing. Remember also that systems will need to be cleaned very thoroughly from time to time so look for a unit that you can disassemble and clean easily. The next chapter will help you understand the details behind the different systems that you can use for gardening. Make sure that you choose the right system since you will be able to obtain all the material you will need for that system.

The drip system

This is one of the most popular systems both for the home gardener and the commercial producer. One of the main reasons that it is so popular is that it facilitates the production of large plants. Basically each plant is potted into growing medium in an individual pot. A drip line is then extended from the reservoir to each pot and when the pump is turned on nutrient solution drips into the pots until such time as the medium is soaked through. The excess solution then drains through the pot to where it is captured in a tray that returns it to the reservoir by means of gravity. The timer is set to turn the pump on again just before the medium gets dry so that the roots are kept constantly moist.

In domestic units these systems tend to be circulating but some commercial units are non- circulating. What happens in these larger operations is that when the water drains through the growing medium it is not captured. This may sound wasteful but it relies on the fact that the timer is so accurate that when set correctly it gives enough solution to the growing medium to wet it exactly with very little waste. Just before the medium dries it then adds more solution. The advantage to the commercial grower is twofold. Firstly, he is not required to have a huge area of catchment trays running the solution back to the reservoir and secondly each time he tops up the reservoir he can replace the exact amount of nutrient appropriate to the plant's needs. The nutrients within a system decrease as they are absorbed by the plant and so a circulating system must be checked frequently to measure the nutrient levels. In a non-circulating system the reservoir must be topped up frequently but on large-scale operations there is normally staff in place to see to this.

Ebb and flow system

This is a method that suits the smaller scale of the domestic user either in the house or in the garden because it is easy to build and can be designed to fit into any available space. Plants are potted into a growing medium and placed into a fairly deep tray. An overflow line is connected to the tray at a level of one or two inches below the surface of the growing medium and water is then pumped from the reservoir into the tray. When the water level reaches the overflow it simply runs back to the reservoir. When this starts a float valve turns off the pump. The same valve turns the water back on again when the reservoir refills. In this way the roots of the plant are constantly being submerged in solution and drained again. It is a system that can be made on a really tiny scale and many pre-made systems utilize this method. When building your own system be sure that the overflow pipe is sufficiently large to carry away water faster than it can arrive via the pump.

Nutrient film technique

In this system plants are grown in a matt of material such as rock wool and placed into a tray with a fine film at its base. A pump carries the nutrients through the film and this soaks the film keeping the roots constantly damp. Excess water simply runs back to the reservoir via gravity. Plants are normally planted through some sort of material to keep light from reaching the roots, as there is no growing medium to cover them.

The system can be very small but when used on large-scale operations long channels are filled with film and the same system is just notched up to a greater size. Because of the shallow depth of this system it is most suited to small fast growing crops such as lettuce and certain types of herb. The system is very effective but with small fast growing plants of this nature there is a risk of them dying quickly in the event of the roots drying out so there is little time to respond if there is some sort of breakdown in the system such as electrical failure.

Water culture system

In this system the root is constantly kept wet by the very fine splashing of tiny droplets of nutrient mix. The plants in are suspended with their roots hanging down into the reservoir. Instead of a water pump an air pump is placed into the reservoir and the water aerated at a pressure that will make the water look like it is boiling lightly. Because the top of the roots are just above the nutrient mix level the bubbling effect created by the pump will cause droplets to hit the roots. This system can be as simple as a large plastic bucket with a hole or holes cut into the lid through which the roots are suspended. The air pump is then placed in the bottom of the bucket and the lid put back on. (You may need to cut a groove for the lead to the pump). The most difficult part of the operation is setting the water depth so that it adequately splashes the roots. Don't worry if the lower roots touch the solution as long as there is still plenty of root material exposed to the air. Make sure that the lid is made of a material that will keep the roots in the dark. This method ensures a really well oxygenated mix reaching the roots but it also requires monitoring of the depth of the solution. More sophisticated systems of the water culture system are used commercially but at the same time it is just an upgrade of the system used by the Aztecs that I mentioned at the beginning of this book.

Aeroponics

Another variation of the hydroponic system is called Aeroponics but as you will see the main principals differ very little from the other techniques you have seen so far. Once again the plants are supported above the solution supply only this time the solution is mist sprayed onto the roots. Like with NFT no growing medium is needed. Think of those small fine sprays you have on an ordinary garden irrigation system. Nutrient solution is pumped from the reservoir and instead of going directly to the routes it passes through the sprayers that wet the roots with a fine mist of water. Excess water can then be captured in trays and run back to the reservoir although the spray spreads the water further and so recapturing the nutrient solution is harder. Most commercial units don't attempt to recapture the moisture but instead try to regulate the delivery system so precisely that there is minimal waste.

The wick system

Of all the systems that have been discussed so far this is by far the simplest one. The plants being grown are potted in their growing medium and then suspended above a bucket of nutrient mix. At its most basic you could have a plastic container with a plant inside balanced on a bucket of nutrients. A wicking material is then placed between the growing medium and the nutrient mix. This can be any material that will carry moisture such as a hemp rope, strips of carpet under-felt or some twisted strips of hessian sacking. There are no moving parts, material costs are minimal, if any, and there is very little skill needed to put it all together.

There are however multiple problems with this method. Firstly only small plans should be grown as the wick, even if you use several, will not be able to carry sufficient water to satisfy the needs of a larger plant. Secondly the wick will not transport the nutrients evenly and those left behind in the reservoir will build up to form a residue that could become toxic to the plant. Thirdly there is no oxygenation taking place in the reservoir. This means could be used by a beginner to grow a few small plants as an introduction to other systems of hydroponics. It is also often used by teachers as a means to demonstrate capillary action, as that is what is taking place here. Some people use an L shaped tube to carry water to the bottom of a plants roots. When the water is poured down the pipe it will be carried upwards by capillary action in the growing medium but this is not really hydroponics in its true sense as devised by Dr. William Gerricke.

There is another system called Aquaponic, which is often confused with hydroponics and does in fact have many similarities but it is not regarded as true hydroponics. Aquaponics principals involve using the waste matter created by fish to feed plants with a system very similar to those of hydroponics. Adding nutrients in controlled quantities is so essential to the philosophy behind hydroponics that the two subjects are best considered separately.

Chapter 6:

Understanding the Hydroponic Systems

This chapter will help you understand the different hydroponics systems much better than you did before. You will gather information on the materials and tools you need to construct the systems. You will also be able to learn how you can make any modifications to the system too!

Bubbler System

This system is the simplest of all hydroponic systems that have ever been developed. It is for this very reason that I am going over this system first. You will be able to build your very own unit using the information that has been given in this section. The system is like a water culture system where the roots are all suspended in the nutrient solution. The system uses the nutrients in the solution to give your plants the boost it needs. The system that has been explained here is only for a few plants.

Material Required

You will need to procure these materials in order to ensure that you build the perfect system.

1. A 10-gallon bucket with a lid. It is always good to get darker colors, but if you have a transparent bucket, you will need to spray paint it with a dark shade.

2. An air pump, stone and tubing. These components are extremely important since they help in sending oxygen into the solution. You could use a small air pump if you want to since that would be enough too.

3. A netted cap. You could choose to purchase a netted cap or you could make it on your own. The size of the cap would depend on the number of plants you would like to cultivate in your system.

4. A growing medium. You could use a nominal amount of one of the media that have been mentioned above.

5. A nutrient mix.

Tools Required

1. A hole saw which is used to adjust the sizes of the netted pots.

2. A power drill that is used to cut the holes in the lid.
3. A tape measure to measure the size of the tubing
4. A drill bit that is used to drill holes in the water gauge and the air tubing.
5. A knife
6. Safety glasses

Construction

1. You will have to make holes in the lid to fit the plastic cups into it. When you are doing this, you have to ensure that the plastic cups are durable and have sides that have tapered. Ensure that the hole is large enough to fit the cup firmly. You have to be certain of the fact that the cups do not slip.
2. You will now have to drill a hole that is perfect to fit in the air tube.
3. Now, move the air tubing through the hole and push it all the way to the bottom of the bucket. You will now have to attach the air stone and leave a few airlines inside the bucket so that the stone will lay flat at the bottom of the bucket.

4. Now fill the bucket with the created nutrient solution. Make sure that the nutrient solution has been prepared according to what crop you will be cultivating. Make sure that it only touches the netted cups and does not submerge them. You will probably have to fill it up with more of the nutrient solution if you are starting with a seed.

5. Cover the bucket with the lid.

6. Once the roots have grown a few inches in the cup, you will need to reduce the level of the nutrient solution at least by an inch at the bottom surface of the plastic cup.

7. Now, hook the other end of the air tube to the air pump and ensure that the nutrient solution begins to bubble.

8. When the bubbles have begun to appear, you will need to place the plant in the netted cups making sure that the roots of the plant only swirl at the bottom of the cup. Now, fill the bottom of the cup with the medium.

9. When the plant has been placed successfully in the medium, you will have to place the cup in the lid of the bucket. There is your system!

Modifications

You will be able to modify the system very easily. If you want, you could add a gauge to measure the water level. This can be done by cutting a half-inch hole on the side of the bucket and inserting a rubber tube of the very same size. Now, connect this tube to an elbow of half an inch and also install a tiny piece of tubing made of vinyl from the top of the bucket.

You could always link your system with a central reservoir or any other source of water using a rubber tube or a grommet. You will need to identify the right fitting methods for the modification.

You could also try to recreate the system by using a variety of materials that are dark in color and also hold a good quantity of water. You should also try to use a material that would help you create more space that would help in holding more plants.

Instructions

You will have to ensure that you monitor the level of water in the system while ensuring that the water level never drops to a point where the plants begin to suffer. You will need to add water to the plants begin to use up all the nutrient solution. When you add water to the bucket, you will need to continue to check the pH and make the adjustments. Make sure that you do not add any fertilizer to the bucket. If you add the fertilizer, you will contaminate the water leading to other problems. You will need to change the nutrient solution when the plants use the nutrient solution completely for the third time.

Ebb and Flow System

The Ebb and Flow system described in the previous chapter is an extremely easy to build and maintain. You will find that the design is extremely flexible and is automated. It is a known fact that plants that have been placed in a growing bed tend to hold a lot of water. The pump in this system is activated through a timer. When the pump is activated, it will pump the nutrient solution into the grow bed from the reservoir. The plants are all watered from the bottom of the reservoir or grow bed. The pump turns off when the plants have been watered for a few seconds. This is done four or five times a day. The system is extremely versatile and is extremely reliable. You will be able to handle the system and the plants really well.

Material needed

1. Air pump, air stone and air tubing
2. Water pump
3. Growing medium – clay or any other cheap medium like gravel

4. Fill and drain

5. Electric timer – 15 minute increments

6. Black irrigation tubing

7. Netted pots

8. Rubbermaid Black Storage Tote w/ Lid – 16 to 20 gallons

9. Rubbermaid Snap-toppers Clear Tote – 28 to 34 quart

10. Water & nutrient mix

Tools needed

1. Hole saw – 1 to ¼" holes

2. Drill bit – needed to drill ½" holes for water gauge and ¼" holes for air tubing

3. Tape measure – for the measurement of tubing sizes

4. Power drill – to cut holes in the lid

5. Teflon tape – for sealing bulkheads

6. Safety glasses

7. Knife – in case you don't have a drill machine

Construction

1. You will first need to cut two holes at the center of the tray that you have collected. You will need to smoothen the edges of the holes and then rub them against sandpaper to smoothen them perfectly. You have to

ensure that the pots you make fit into the holes you have just made. You have to ensure that you have a rough estimate of the size of the hole in your mind before you make the holes.

2. When you have successfully cut the drain holes in the tray, you will need to place the tray over the tote lid. Make sure that the tray is at the center of the tote lid. You will need to mark the center of the holes you have created onto the lid. Make sure that you have marked it well. The idea is that the holes you have made and the drain fittings overlap each other properly.

3. You will now have to cut two more holes into the lid – one of these holes is for the pump plug and the other is to measure the level of the nutrient solution and also add more of the nutrient solution when the level of the solution falls.

4. You will now have to place the drain fittings into the holes that are at the center of the clear container. You will need to place the rubber gasket at the bottom of the bin and screw it in tightly. It is best to use your hands for this since tools make it extremely difficult to hold onto the screws tightly.

5. You will need to place the irrigation tube over the outlet fitting of the pump. The securing mechanism is directly affected by the type of hosing you would be using in the system. It is possible that you may need to use a zip tie.

6. You will need to place the container that has been fitted with the drains in line with the holes that

4. Rubber grommets

5. 4 inch PVC pipes of 10 inch lengths, cut into 3 portions

6. 4 straight connectors

7. 5 gallon bucket or container or Aquaponics fish tank

8. 1 x submersible pump

9. Air pumps, tubing & stones

10. 3 inch netted cups

11. ½ inch – ¾ inch irrigation tubing

12. Hydroponic nutrient

Tools needed

1. Utility knife

2. 3 inch hole saw

3. Screws Drill

4. Saw

5. Standard screwdriver

Construction

1. When you have decided on the type of container you would be using for the reservoir, you will need to start with the design for your stands. What you will need to remember is that the design of the stands

must be done well to ensure that they are taller than the reservoir itself.

2. You will need to cut the lengths of the stand and cut a triangle out of the lengths. This is to ensure that the PVC can be held in a stable position. You will then need to join the lengths well using the other stands by placing them horizontally.

3. You will now have to drill a hole in order to make space for the tubing. This is to ensure that the tube connects to the caps well. You will need to drill these holes in the heights where you want the water to stay. You have to also ensure that the holes are at a height where you would be able to ensure that the water does not submerge the cups. You could also make the holes adjustable if you want to. This can be done by drilling a hole on the outside of the fitting in order to adjust the level of water using the rubber fitting.

4. When you are purchasing the pump, you will need to ensure that it comes with an attachment that can be removed easily. This will be required since you will need to bind this to the piece of tubing in order to reach the top of the tube right from the bottom of the reservoir.

5. You will now need to push the tubes from the bottom to the NFT fitting through the created hole. You will need to use another piece of the tubing along with the NFT in order to reach the top of the tube. You will have to do the

same with the bottom of the tube and the reservoir. You will now have to attach the caps together till they fit well on the pieces of the PVC.

6. The NFT system always runs well and if there are any leaks, you will be able to use the plumbing cement on the outside of the tubes. When looked from the perspective of toxicity, you will find that the plumbing cement is not the best one to use. It is only good to use it on the outside of your system. You will find that you can conduct another leak test in an hour tops!

7. If you are someone who loves keeping every single item clean, you will need to sue a bleach solution to clean the reservoir and every other material before you drill any holes. This is to ensure that you maximize the flow that is within the tubes.

8. The next thing you will need to do is that you will need to drill the holes in the system that would be dependent on the type and the size of the plant. It is always good to make space for 6 – 9 plants. Make sure that you maintain at least 6inhches between each plant that you cultivate. You would do great by drilling the holes for the plants using the netter cups. You could also use plastic cups, but ensure that you are in a safe place. You will need to wear a mask to ensure that you do not harm yourself. You will need to remove all the dust off of the pipes.

9. You will need to make three holes in the lid covering the reservoir where each of the holes would have its own purpose. You will need to use one for the supply of water, one for the drain and the other for the air tubing or the power cord.

10. You will need to leave the lid on top of the reservoir to ensure that the evaporation is reduced. You will also be able to protect your plants from any debris that may fall into the container.

11. You could choose to either use the netted pots that are available in the market or use the homemade netter pots. When you purchase them, you will be able to use the pots immediately. If you are making it at home, you will need to drill a lot of holes to ensure that the cups work well. You will need to make sure that the roots fit well through the holes in order to be submerged into the nutrient solution.

12. The lower part of the tubing must always be directed to that side of the reservoir where there is light – natural or artificial. You have to check the stands to ensure that you have the right orientation of the flow of water. The water needs to move from the top of the stands to the bottom and back into the reservoir.

13. When you have chosen a growing medium, you have to ensure that it is clean and has been sterilized well. This needs to be done to ensure that you do not contaminate the system with

pests. If you are willing to purchase a medium from the store, you will only need to clean the dust or the debris.

14. When you are moving the plant from the soil into the reservoir, you will need to remove any soil particles from the plant. This is to avoid any clogging since that will harm the plants. Make sure that the plant is clean too.

Make sure that you place the taller plants at the back and the shorter ones in front to ensure that each plant receives the right amount of sunlight.

There are four factors that have an extreme influence on the workings of the NFT system.

- The number of plants
- The size of the channel tubing
- The specifications of the channel
- The capability of the pump

The best thing to do is to use a pump that is not too small. This is because of the fact that the solution may not be drained too easily. It would also affect the motor extremely badly. You will be able to transform the system extremely easily if you choose to. You can always experiment with the system in order to obtain the best out of it. You have learnt a great deal of the NFT system, but the modifications are always endless. You could always cut the tube into the same length to ensure that the plants have been fed well.

Chapter 7:

Nutrient Solutions

G etting the correct nutrients to the roots of your plants roots is what hydroponics is all about. The science behind plant nutrition is quite complicated and at first can seem very daunting but it is not necessary to become a plant scientist to get to grips with what you will need to know in order to be a successful grower. It will, however, help to know some of the basics so you have an idea of what is going on and what all those chemicals are.

There are many different nutrients that a plant requires in order to grow and without which they will soon die. The three main nutrients are called macronutrients whilst an array of other nutrients are needed but in much smaller quantities.

The three-macro nutrients are:

Nitrogen (N): used in the production of chlorophyll and amino acids.

Phosphate (P): used in the production of sugars, energy flowers and fruit.

Potassium (K): used in the production of sugars starch, roots and general hardiness.

These three components are always listed most prominently on bottles or packets of nutrients and given in numbers proportional to their quantity so if you were to see 15:9:12 you would know their proportions were fifteen percent Nitrogen, nine percent Phosphate and twelve percent Potassium. That would make up thirty six percent of the mix with the remainder being given over to water and micronutrients. It should be noted that the three figures are always given in the same order NPK although the percentage of each will vary according to its intended usage.

In hydroponics the nutrients most commonly supplied come in a powdered or a concentrated liquid form that you would then dilute according to instructions of the manufacturer. In my opinion, and that of many other growers, the liquid form is by far the most practical and easy to use.

As I have already mentioned the reservoir should be a tank that does not let in light so as to reduce the possibility of mold and algae build up. This reservoir should be at least the same size as the pots or tray that it is feeding and possibly bigger. Don't mix the nutrients in the reservoir but add them after premixing with water.

The pH level of your water is very important as it can have a detrimental effect on the nutrient take up if it is either too high or too low. Ideally you want it to be at between 5.5 and 7.0. Too much chlorine can also have adverse effects so that too will need to be dealt with. If you stand water in a bucket for twenty-four hours the chlorine will breakdown. Alternatively, you can buy distilled water that seems a bit of a waste of money to me or you can catch rainwater, which will be chlorine free and seems to me the most logical solution to the chlorine problem. Don't be too distracted by chlorine levels as they don't kill plants and water that has stood for twenty-four hours tends to be fine.

The pH is most commonly affected by the amount of calcium it contains. Too much calcium leads to hard water and a high pH. This will need to be tested with a pH tester and if it falls outside of the given range then you can add some drops of a chemical for raising it or another for lowering it depending on the reading you are getting. All hydroponic suppliers sell a two-part kit for raising and lowering pH. Simply dilute a few drops of one or the other in order to either raise or lower the pH to the required level. Do this mixing in a little at a time and then let the water settle before testing again. It is good to have a general idea of the pH of you water when you first start but after that most of the pH testing should be done after you have added the various nutrients, as these will further alter the pH levels. The digital testing devise, a bit like a thermometer, is quite cheap and simple to use.

One way to make your life easier is to have a second reservoir. One will be in use and the other will be full with just water. This will ensure that the water is at the same temperature so the plants don't have to deal with a sudden temperature change and will also mean you are free of any chlorine if using mains tap water. Try to always use tepid water at around 18°C but don't make this a major issue as you are going to have enough to get to grips with at the moment.

Once you have your water more or less pH neutral it is time to start mixing your nutrients and for the moment I am only going to deal with purpose bought hydroponic nutrients. They normally come in three parts that are mixed according to the manufacturer's instructions for the plants that you are growing. They tend to come with a chart for a range of plants and with a week-by-week dosage according to the age of the plants. In the beginning you will want to follow this chart quite closely but as your experience levels increase you will no doubt start experimenting with recipes of your own. Almost all hydroponic gardeners develop their individual recipes and start to add a series of additional products that they all swear are the best for the plants they hope to produce. I will get into some of those additives late but for now we will just stick to mixing of the basic three part nutrients.

Once you have the three bottles and have found the appropriate part of the chart that applies to your plants and the stage of growth they are at you will need to mix them. Don't just throw them all into a jar and shake them all up. In strong concentration they can react with one another and create an effect called blocking that inhibits their individual effectiveness. Instead place a few liters of water in a bucket that is the same size as your reservoir. This water will need to be chlorine free and to the correct pH. Of course if you have the second reservoir already prepared then that will be perfect. Pour the correct amount of the first nutrient into a measuring beaker and then pour it into the water. Now wash out the beaker and wait two minutes before repeating the procedure with the second nutrient. Finally repeat the process with the third nutrient. Remember it is important that you wash out the measuring beaker between nutrients to avoid blocking. It is also possible to purchase some cheap measuring syringes and use a separate one for each nutrient so as to avoid any possibility of mixing them up.

Once I have all my nutrients in the reservoir and I have waited a minute or two after adding the three then I give the reservoir a bit of a stir. At this stage I can retest my pH to ensure the levels are still within the accepted range of 5.5 to 7.0. It is likely that over time the pH will creep up slightly as the nutrients are drawn up by the plant. Because this is the case it would be good if you could keep the pH just slightly below neutral so if you can keep it to around 6.0 that would be ideal. I then also test my mix using another meter called a PPM meter or an EC meter and occasionally a TDC meter. Effectively they all do the same thing. They measure the salts in the nutrient mix. PPM stands for parts per million, EC stands for Electrical conductivity and TDS stands for total desired salts. This easy to use little gadget will be used often during the growing stage, as you will need to be constantly monitoring your nutrient mix to ensure the plant is getting all that it needs. Getting to grips with nutrient mixes is one of the trickiest parts of hydroponic gardening and I don't want to make it appear too complicated because you can generally learn all you need to by just following the chart that comes with the mixture. Remember that each producer will have a different recipe and so each system will vary slightly.

What you are trying to do with the plant varies at different times of its growth cycle and that is why the mixture of ingredients keeps altering. To start off you want plenty of nitrogen to bring the plants to a flowering stage as soon as possible. Later you will reduce the nitrogen but increase the phosphates to increase the flowering rooting and fruiting and all the way through the process you plant will be in need of small amounts of micronutrients. In the early days there will normally be a strong desire to add more nutrients in the hope that this will generate more and faster growth. In fact, too much nutrient can be worse for the plant than too little nutrient so if you must tamper with the manufacturers recommendations try to always err on the side of less rather than more.

Now you have got your reservoir to the pH you want and the nutrients to the level recommended by the manufacturer you are set to start pumping. Most systems require circulation at least twice a day and if you can get that up to once every two hours without water logging the plants that would be even better. You should be using your meter to check the nutrients every couple of days. If they start to get low then you can add a top up mix that is essentially a mild version of the mixes you are using without the micronutrients. The reason for this is that the plants use a lot of the macronutrients and only very little of the micronutrients. If you add more micronutrient it builds up in the system and becomes toxic to the plants. Outdoor units must not be exposed to rain that will dilute the water in the system.

Every two weeks you should replace the nutrient mix altogether. It is safe to pour the old mix onto any soil garden plants you have. Before making up the next mix clean out the reservoir with hot water or diluted bleach. You are then ready to start a new batch provided the water is chlorine free. This is also a good time to check the rest of the system to check that everything is working and there is no sign of algae. Pay particular attention to mist heads if you are using them as they are easily blocked up by micronutrient build up.

Although I have suggested checking your unit you should be checking your plants every day to ensure that they are strong and healthy and not showing any signs of stress. They will also let you know very quickly if there is any problem with the system. When you have harvested your crop then it is a good idea to strip the entire unit down and give everything a thorough cleansing. When you go a little ahead in this chapter, you will come across recipes you could use to make your nutrient solution and will also be able to identify the easiest ways to test the pH of the water in the reservoir.

The intricate nutrient solution

Before I move on to explain to you the intricacies of the nutrient solution, let me tell you a little about the strength of a plant. You could try to visualize the plant as a chain. The strength of the plant is similar to the strength of a chain.

You may have come across the proverb, 'A chain is as strong as its weakest link'. This implies that your chain is always as strong if its links are all strong too! You will therefore have to ensure that every link is stable and has a good supply. You have to make sure that you only add the right quantity of the nutrients to the solution. You will also need to ensure that you understand your plants better since every plant will have a requirement of its own.

The nutrients that you will need are all available in the market and always come with a set of instructions about the proportions you will need to mix to obtain the final solution. You have to also understand what type of a solution you will need for your plant during the different stages of germination. You will find a ton of products in the market that you could use in the different systems of hydroponics. You may be a beginner and it may be easier for you to use the readymade solutions. But, if you choose to make nutrients for your plants, you could use the recipes at the end of the chapter to do the same!

When you have made a list of all the ingredients together, you will have to be careful about a few things. What is of great importance is that you need to design the solution in such a way that the hydroponics system works well. Make sure that you do not use any supplements at all in the system. This is because of the fact that the medium you use to grow your plants in do not have any microorganisms. Since they are not available, the nutrients from the supplements will not be transferred to the plants. You could choose to use certain powders if you want to, but ensure that they have multi purposes. Ensure that you use these powders only when there is extremely poor lighting.

If the location you have chosen to place your hydroponic system is under direct sunlight, ensure that you use a powder with at least two functions. This will ensure that the yield of the plants will multiply. This is because of an extremely simple reason. Multipurpose nutrients always ensure that they satisfy the needs of each one of your plants. You will be unable to bend the uses of the powders to satisfy the needs of one single plant. The second reason behind why it is good for you to use multipurpose nutrient powders is that blending the powders together would work best since that would imply that the plants have been given all the nutrients that they require. The best way to do this is by optimizing the growth of your plants by using this method.

There are a few people who would want to prepare their own nutrient solution. A few recipes have been given below and if want to prepare your own nutrients, you will need to follow these recipes word for word. These powders can be used at the different stages of germination.

Recipes for Nutrients

Let us look at a few recipes if you are keen on preparing your own nutrient solutions.

Vegetative Nutrient

Amount: 4 liters

Nitrogen: 38

Phosphorous: 24

Potassium: 48

Ingredients

- 24 lb. Calcium Nitrate
- 88 lb. Potassium Nitrate
- 122 lb. Sulfate of Potash
- 8 lb. Monopotassium Phosphate
- 10 lb. Magnesium Sulfate
- 4 lb. Fe Chelated Trace Elements

Instructions

Mix these ingredients separately and add the powder to four gallons of water.

Fruiting Nutrient

Amount: 4 liters

Nitrogen: 32

Phosphorous: 22

Potassium: 50

Ingredients

- 32 lb. Calcium Nitrate
- 10 lb. Potassium Nitrate
- 8 lb. Sulfate of Potash
- 6 lb. Monopotassium Phosphate
- 12 lb. Magnesium Sulfate
- 4 lb. Fe Chelated Trace Elements

Instructions

Mix these ingredients separately and add the powder to four gallons of water.

Flowering Nutrient

Amount: 4 liters

Nitrogen: 22

Phosphorous: 32

Potassium: 74

Ingredients

- 20 lb. Calcium Nitrate
- 10 lb. Potassium Nitrate
- 4 lb. Sulfate of Potash
- 8 lb. Monopotassium Phosphate
- 10 lb. Magnesium Sulfate
- 2 lb. Fe Chelated Trace Elements

Instructions

Mix these ingredients separately and add the powder to four gallons of water.

The secrets behind the chelated trace elements

The chelated trace elements have an amazing combination that is unique. The first thing for you to do is to understand these combinations since that will ensure that you make the right combination of the nutrient solution if that is what you want to do. You will need to ensure that the combination is right since an excess would harm the plants in ways you would never have imagined.

1. Molybdenum – 0.06%
2. Manganese – 2%
3. Copper – 0.1%
4. Iron – 7%
5. Zinc – 0.4%
6. Boron – 1.30%

General instructions

When you have decided to make the nutrient solutions for your hydroponics system on your own, you will need to follow a few instructions that are extremely important. Please read this section carefully to go over those rules.

The first thing you will need to do is to fill the reservoir or two reservoirs with extremely clean and hot water. You will only have to fill the reservoir to three fourths of the capacity. Now, add the nutrients that have been given above in the recipes. Make sure that you add them one after the other since that way you will be able to ensure that the nutrients have mixed well with the system. This is extremely important.

Make sure that you remember the fact that the salts are in their native states that would mean that there is a possibility of them having a strong reaction. You will need to keep yourself protected well. Ensure that you always follow the instructions that have been given for every nutrient you will be using.

How do you test the pH of the nutrient solution?

When you are adding the nutrient solution to your reservoir, you will have to ensure that you measure the pH of the solution. You could use two techniques – TDS (Total Dissolved Solids) and PPM (Parts Per Million) – for the same. You would have come across the term electrical conductivity that is the very same thing. I have said this since you will be measuring the electrical conductivity of the nutrient solution that you have made.

You could use multiple ways to analyze and measure the PPM of any nutrient solution. The simplest way to do this is by using a digital PPM gauge. In order to take the measurement, you will need to place the gauge in the solution. The best part of this is that you do not have to calibrate the gauge. If you always change the nutrient solution the concentration and the pH are always at the level needed. The best thing for you to do is to follow every instruction that has been given on the back of the nutrient you will be using. It is always good to replace the solution at least once every three weeks if you are keen on obtaining good results.

It is an absolute waste to have a nutrient solution in the reservoir if you find that that the plant cannot absorb the nutrients easily. In order to understand the ability of a plant to absorb all the nutrients that are in the solution, you will have to gauge the pH of the nutrient solution. It is always measured on a scale of 1 -14 and always represents the number of hydrogen ions in the nutrient solution. The pH is always good to try to understand the nature of the solution – whether or not it is basic or acidic. If the scale is one you will find that the concentration of the hydrogen ion is extremely low, while if it is a seven it means that the solution is neutral. If the scale says 14, you will find that the solution is alkaline or basic. You could also use a simple litmus test if you want, just how you did it in chemistry class.

To Recap

By now you may be starting to feel like you have been bombarded with a little too much information especially if hydroponics is something you have never dealt with before.

The whole idea is to ensure that you get a nutrient rich liquid to the roots of your plants with a nearly neutral pH. If you focus on those priorities you won't go too far wrong. To do this you will need an EC meter for the salts or nutrients and a pH meter. You can buy fairly inexpensive units that do both measurements for you so checking the levels is not difficult. You should be checking your mixture once a day. Small scale units tend to fluctuate more than larger ones so the home grower has to be just as alert to changes as the large scale producer.

In the event of pH getting too high or too low then add a few drops of the appropriate product after diluting. There are two products you can buy for this and they clearly state that they are either for raising or lowering the pH. You should not try to change the pH more than 0.5 in either direction in one day as you may shock the plants. As you started with the right pH balance larger changes are unlikely.

The EC meter will give you a reading of the conductivity of the water based on the amount of salts that it contains. Aim for a level of between 1.2 and 2.0. If it goes above this you can dilute the mix by adding water and if it goes below then you can top it up with top up according to the manufacturer's instructions. I hope that simplifies this chapter for you.

Chapter 8:

What to Grow

One of the great advantages of hydroponics is the wide variety of crops that you can grow. In many ways the choice is endless but you do need to take into consideration the constraints imposed on you by the size of your unit and the space that it is in. If you are a large producer in a greenhouse set up you will probably want to concentrate on a small range of crops that sell easily and if you are a home grower working in an apartment then perhaps it is best to focus on just the crops that you buy most of. For the small producer a good place to start is always with lettuce as it is a salad crop that is eaten by ninety percent of westerners on a daily basis. It is also a crop that takes up little space and really tastes better freshly picked. In addition you can also harvest enough leaves for a salad whilst leaving the plant to continue growing.

The second most popular crop is tomato. If there is one crop that tastes better than all others when picked and eaten immediately then it has to be the tomato. There are hundreds of varieties so choose one that you think you will enjoy and that takes up not too much space. If possible grow two plants of different varieties that will produce at different times so that you can harvest for a longer period. If you are combining your hydroponics with grow lights and growing indoors then it is possible to have tomatoes virtually all year round.

Cucumbers are another plant that can be very rewarding. In an indoor environment go for a dwarf variety and have a frame up which they can climb.

Peppers are not only easy to grow they also make surprisingly attractive plants especially if they are the brightly colored varieties. Another crop we use on a regular basis in our homes so an instant saving there.

Spinach is one of the most popular leaf vegetables and is very high in vitamins and iron. These days there are many varieties ranging from those with small rounded leaves through to the more traditional longer leaved ones. All of them can have some leaves harvested whilst leaving the parent plant to continue growing and reproducing new leaves.

For fruit strawberries are one of the best fruit for the hydroponic producer in both the private and commercial environments. With the vastly extended growing season you will have, the potential for good economic returns are high.

Blue berries are going through a major popularity boom at the moment because of their high levels of antioxidants that have proven health benefits. They like an acid soil when growing in the ground and as it is so easy to control acidity in a hydroponic production unit this makes them solid candidates for both home and commercial production.

Herbs can be surprisingly expensive when you actually work out what quantities you get when you buy them in a supermarket. Growing your own makes sense and even if you are only intending to grow enough for you and your family it is possible that you may find that you are producing more than you can eat. If you ask around it is highly likely that you will find ready buyers amongst your family and neighbors. Basil is used in a number of recipes as an addition to salads. It is also high in antioxidants. A very easy to grow herb, it costs a small fortune in supermarkets when you look at the price per kilogram.

The other really easy to grow herb is coriander. With its many health benefits and multiple culinary uses this is a versatile crop that you can be harvesting within four weeks and which can easily provide two and sometimes three crops per year.

Chapter 9:

Pests and Diseases

There is one sure thing about any form of gardening and that is that you will always run into problems with pests and disease at some stage or other. In the case of hydroponics the problem of pests is reduced considerably because your crop is not growing in the soil where many bugs tend to lay their eggs and hibernate. Unfortunately, that still does not mean that you will be totally immune to receiving attention from nasty creatures as those healthy looking leaves and fruit will be just too much for them to resist and they will find other ways of getting at an easy meal.

One of the most important lessons any gardener learns is that of observation. Bugs and insects have developed various defense mechanisms and the main one is the ability to blend into their environment so that they can go unnoticed for as long as possible. Another survival strategy is to breed very rapidly. The gardener needs to almost cultivate a sixth sense when it comes to spotting pests. A casual glance will see only a healthy looking lettuce but the trained eye will soon spot one or two tiny aphids lurking hidden beneath the leaves. If they are dealt with swiftly then the problem has been averted but left to their own devices those few aphids can breed to almost plague proportions within a matter of days and suddenly you whole harvest is at risk and getting rid of them now demands all-out war. Take the time to look closely at your plants, turning over leaves and using a magnifying glass if you need to. Also learn to recognize when a plant is not looking one hundred percent healthy and is displaying even the slightest signs of stress.

Here are some of the most common pests you are likely to encounter.

Mealy Bug

An oval shaped scale insect that sucks sap from the veins of leaves. They produce a sticky substance known as honey dew that often gives away their presence. They can be dealt with by wiping with rubbing alcohol on a cotton ball or spraying with an insecticidal soap.

Spider Mites

These tiny insects are almost invisible to the naked eye and they thrive in green house conditions. You often only become aware of them when you see a fine web covering the underside of leaves and the base of leaves starts to become a mottled brown as they suck out the chlorophyll. In small infestations caught early they may be destroyed simply by misting the leaves with a mild soapy solution. Use vegetable based insecticidal soap if they get out of control.

Thrips

Small winged insects a little larger than the head of a pin and they too like to suck sap. Leaves become distorted and loose color. They are best dealt with by spraying with soapy water.

Aphids

There are various types of aphid but they all have one thing in common and that is that they can breed really fast. It is estimated that if all the offspring from a single aphid were to survive for a year then their combined body weight would be sufficient to throw the earth out of orbit. Fortunately for us they are quite fragile creatures and if you spot them early they can be dealt with before we go spinning off toward another universe. They are sapsuckers and tend to favor the tips of green leaves. They are easily destroyed by a quick blast of soapy spray.

This is a very short list of some of the most common pests but there are many more and many varieties of the ones that I have listed. What I was trying to emphasize is that they are easy to deal with if you catch them early. Given that most of the plants you are growing are likely to be edible then you need to decide if you are going to treat your pests with chemicals or organic treatments. Organic pest control tends to be cheaper and as I don't want to expose myself to any more toxic chemicals than I need to I tend to opt for them. There is, however, a vast array of chemical sprays and treatments on the market that are highly effective at killing any pest you care to mention and you only have to go into a garden center and describe your problem and you will be offered a selection of arms with which to respond.

On the organic front the arsenal is more limited but here are some of the treatments that have worked perfectly well for me.

Insecticidal soaps can be sprayed from an ordinary spray bottle and are my weapon of choice. You can purchase them or make up your own using any number of recipes off the net using common household ingredients.

Neem oil is produced from an evergreen tree that originates in India and is now grown widely around the world. Its oil is prized by both the organic gardening and cosmetic industry. It will be available at most nurseries or online.

Nettle tea. This is a product that any gardener who has access to nettles can make himself. Simply steep a large handful of nettles in lightly simmering water for five minutes then filter the greenish brown liquid into a spray bottle. It gets more powerful as it ages and is a great insect deterrent but beware, as it does smell.

On the disease front the main threat comes from high humidity and the close density of planting that is common in the hydroponic system. This makes growers, particularly greenhouse producers, susceptible to molds and mildews of which there are many. The secret is to increase ventilation as much as possible and to reduce humidity down to the lowest levels your plants will accept.

Both pests and disease are reduced if you practice good garden hygiene. Remove and throw away dead plants and leaves immediately. Thoroughly clean and disinfect all equipment between crops as well as green houses. Use tools specifically for the hydroponic system so as to avoid unintentionally carry in disease spores from other plants in the garden. If you are using grow lights then don't be tempted to share the light with other house plants that you may have as you risk transfer problems.

Chapter 10:

What are the Benefits of Hydroponic Gardening?

Numerous people have started to work towards hydroponic gardening instead of using conventional methods of gardening. The only problem that you may have with this sort of arrangement is that the plants may not have the ability to keep themselves free of pests. You have been given a detailed explanation on how you can get rid of the pests if you find your system affected by them.

It has been seen that people all across the world have started to become extremely conscious about the food they are consuming. They have started to consume organic food. Here is the thing: not all organic food is good since you will not be able to know the method of cultivation that has been used. There are numerous people who have always stated that they have produced organic food when in reality they are producing regular food – that is food with pesticides and fertilizers. This is because of the fact that they will begin to focus on the returns they will be obtaining. You will need to be extremely careful when you are purchasing the organic food.

When you switch over to using a hydroponics system instead of using the conventional farming method, you will find that you cannot cheat at all. You have to ensure that you do not use even one chemical in your system since that will affect the growth of all the plants in the system. If you begin to use any pesticides or fertilizers in your system, the plants in the reservoir will begin to wither. Make sure that you do not have even one chemical for this very reason. The best part is that you will be able to produce organic food since you are never allowed to use any chemicals, even if they are organic!

The most important thing you will need to keep in your mind is that the hydroponics system does not need any chemical at all to function well. The system works towards creating a harmony between the different elements of nature. The fertilizers you provide to the plants in your system are all natural and found in the nutrient solution. This will ensure that your plants grow very well.

Other Benefits

Let us look at a few other benefits that you will obtain when you use hydroponic systems.

Farming

The greatest benefit of all is that you will obtain a great deal of knowledge on effective techniques of farming. You will be able to obtain a yield that is either thrice or four times the yield you may obtain when you try to use the conventional methods of farming.

When you begin to use the land you own to cultivate your plants traditionally, you will find yourself wasting a lot of water. The water that you will use to cultivate your plants would often be used to clean the soil and will end up seeping deep into the soil. An extremely minute amount of water is absorbed by the roots of your plant. You could probably be wondering why I am saying this since you would be using a lot of water in the hydroponic system. The fact is that the water in the system is always circulated around the roots of the plant that would ensure that the water never goes to waste.

You will find that you do not have the need to pull any weeds out of the hydroponic system since every plant always grows extremely well since the medium used in the system is extremely controlled. The plants in the hydroponic system always grow faster than the plants that have been cultivated using traditional techniques. This is always due to the fact that the nutrient solution that contains every mineral and vitamin your plant needs. This would imply that you do not have to work hard or even spend a lot of money! You only need to have the right proportions of the nutrients before you pour it into the reservoir.

Environment

Fertilizers and pesticides have tons of chemicals in them that would often lead to harming the ground water, which is because of the fact that the chemicals seep through the ground. This would lead to polluting the larger water bodies that are connected to the ground water table. When you start using a hydroponic system at home, you will find that you do not need any fertilizers and pesticides. This is because of the fact that you will be using a nutrient solution to keep all your plants healthy. The food you obtain thereof is extremely important.

The other aspect to consider about the environment is the land. People have been using all the land they can find! When you use a hydroponic system, you will be able to conserve a lot of pieces of land. This is because of the fact that you will need extremely small amounts of space to start and maintain your hydroponic system.

Health

The plants that have been cultivated in the system are extremely healthy. There are no chemicals that are inserted in the system that would mean that the plants are chemical free. The only way the plants obtain their health is through the nutrient solutions that are made. The organic fertilizers are often obtained from animals, which contain a certain pathogen that would harm the plants extremely badly.

Chapter 11:

Grooming of the Plants

People are always worried about how they can make sure that their plants are healthy and do not become prey for certain pests and insects. This is when they, including you, will need to learn a little something about grooming. There are four techniques to grooming your plants. You have to use these methods carefully in order to ensure that you do not hurt the delicate plants. It is a fact that the plants that grow in the system are delicate although they are strong to handle any climatic changes. This however, does not mean that your plants will be attacked by a variety of pests. You may make mistakes initially, but that is alright since you will begin to learn from those mistakes. Make sure that you keep yourself motivated and are forging ahead in your journey.

Pinching

This is an extremely simple technique and it is essential that you are extremely careful with the delicate plants. You have to use your thumb and forefinger to hold the part of the plant you will be cutting gently but firmly. This method will help you keep all your plants compact and extremely clean and neat.

You will always be able to use this method to retain the structure of the plant. You have to always keep in mind that you pinch above a node since you do not want to harm your plant. You could use this method for plants that have a very soft stem. If you cannot use this method, you will need to use the next method.

Pruning

Make sure that the pruner shears that you will be using to trim all the edges of the plants are sharp. This is because of the fact that the stems you will be cutting are wood. You will have to use the prunes to get rid of any parts of the plant that have been injured, even if it is a small injury, you will need to remove that part. Make sure you do this to avoid giving your plants any diseases. During the spring season, you will need to do this more frequently since your plants will begin to grow extremely fast!

Deadheading Flowers

If there are any dry or dead flowers or even dry leaves, you will need to remove them. This is to avoid the growth of mold, which often causes and spreads numerous diseases.

Cleaning

Make sure that you always keep your hydroponic system extremely clean. It is only when there is no dust in the system will you be able to attract the right amount of sunlight which will keep your plants strong and will help them grow well. Ensure that you clean your leaves and flowers using a damp cloth. Also ensure that you are extremely gentle!

Tips and Tricks!

When you decide to use a hydroponics system at home, you will be looking for ways to make your life easier. This section will thrill you since it holds a treasure of tips that will help you through your journey. You may be overwhelmed at times when you find that there are multiple things you will need to remember and take care of while you are working on the system. Worrying only makes it worse! All you need to do is enjoy what you are doing and you will be perfectly fine!

1. You have to ensure that the equipment you will be using for the system has been washed well before it is placed in the hydroponics system. Make sure that no dirt enters the system since that makes it a little more work for you. You will need to remove the dirt and then use the system.

2. When you are trying to identify the different media you can use in the hydroponics system, the first thing you will need to check is the pH. Make sure that the medium does not cause any fluctuations in the pH of the system since that would affect the plants adversely.

3. When you are trying to analyze the water in your surroundings, you will probably find that the water contains too much protein. This will need to be removed immediately before you use it in your system.

4. You need to ensure that the nutrient solution you make always has the right quantity of minerals and vitamins. If you have too much of the nutrients, you will be affecting the growth of the plants. The same can be said for a low amount of nutrients in the solution.

5. You need to remember to always use products made from nature. This is to ensure that chemicals do not make their way into your hydroponics system. If they enter the system then they will be absorbed by the plants that would harm them internally.

6. It is possible that your plants could be affected by a variety of pests. These need to be removed soon to avoid harming your plants or the entire system. You could always use a spray made of water and vinegar that you can use on your plants if you find them affected by pests.

7. If you have any plants out in the open, you have to ensure that there is a protective covering over them. You will be able to keep them from any harm they may come across if they are out in the open. You will also be able to keep them away from the birds and other pests.

Chapter 12:

The Requirements for a Hydroponics System

The hydroponics systems are always easy to use and are extremely easy to develop. There are a few conditions and requirements that will need to be met by a hydroponics system in order to obtain a high yield. You have been given a list of all these conditions in order to recall them easily.

- You have to ensure that the pH of the nutrient solution lies between the values 5.8 – 6.5 while the electrical conductivity must lie between the values 1.5 - 2.5. If every plant is subjected to these conditions, the yield will be very high. If there were a sudden change, it would harm the plants in the system terribly.
- It is extremely vital that you monitor the temperature of the nutrient solution in the tank. When the temperature increases, the rate of respiration also increases which would increase the demand for oxygen. If you place the hydroponics system in a greenhouse, you will find that

the temperature has increased too much and is at its peak in the afternoon!

- There will be a lot of oxygen that has been dissolved in the nutrient solution in order to ensure that the roots of the plants can absorb it. If there is a reduced amount of oxygen it will mean that the rate of absorption has also decreased. This will have a direct impact on the yield of the crops. If the system is closed, you will find that the collection of the nutrient solution will allow for the aeration of the tank.

- If you are using root-dipping techniques, you will need to give way for an air gap that is nominal. This will need to be measure with respect to the nutrient solution. The roots will be absorbing the oxygen for the plants and will help the plants grow well together in the same system.

- You have to make changes to the nutrient solution, but ensure that you do not make sudden changes since that will affect the growth of the plants.

- When the crop is growing, you will find that the concentration of the ions is decreasing in the nutrient solution. You will find that the decrease of the ions is inversely proportional to the nutrient solution level. If there is an increase, you will find that it is not healthy for the plants. You will need to remove the solution and add the newer solution to the reservoir.

- Since you are growing plants in a medium without soil, you will need to ensure that there is adequate light.

- Any seedlings that can be used to avoid pests and diseases will need to be used when you are trying to establish the hydroponics crops. You will have to remove any plant if it has been infected or harmed. If you do not do this, you will be inviting pests to your system.

- If you come across a nematode problem when you use solid media, you will need to empty the system – remove the plants and the media. You will now have to sterilize the media and replace it if you still doubt the quality of the media. You have to also ensure that there are no nematodes in the water.

- Algae will begin to develop in the system as time passes and will tend to block the passageway making it difficult for the system to provide the plants with the nutrient solution. In order to avoid such a problem, you will need to use dark shades of pipes and also maintain an extremely clean system. Also make sure that the solution has absolutely no chlorine in it.

- You have to make sure that you have a good amount of spacing between the crops you will be placing in the reservoir. This is to ensure that each plant gets its fair share of nutrients.

- You will need to make sure that there is an adequate amount of nutrients that are needed to maintain the yield of the crops. You have to therefore, ensure that every plant gets a little bit of each of these elements. You will need to ensure that the nutrient solution is in the right amount since that is the only way you will be able to ensure a better yield.

Conclusion

I hope that some of the technicalities here have not put you off what can be a very rewarding field of horticulture. In the beginning it may seem a little overwhelming but as you start to work with the different systems and methods you will find that you begin to get a feel for the subject. In gardening terms this is still a fairly new method and we are all still learning as the system evolves. There are some really cheap and easy methods for you to experiment with and once you have seen how straightforward hydroponics really is and how much bigger a yield can be achieved then I am sure you will want to move up to greater things. This system is already being used to produce many of the crops we buy at the supermarket and eat on a day to day basis and there is no reason why you should not be doing some of that production for your own home and perhaps from there even looking to expand toward bigger things.